Moravie

belochrobates

Presbourg

Unghwar

Provence

Corse

Avignon

Arles

Aix

Gênes

Florence
et ITALIE
Toscane

Ravenne

Pentapole

Ancône

Spolète

Uleria

Iladera

Spalatre

ROME

Sardaigne

M.t Cassin

Raguse

Dalm

Cagliari

Bénévent
Naples

Bénévent
p.te

Bari

Salerne
p.te

Tarente

Dyrra

Otrante

Bone

Biserte

Palerme

Sicile

Calabre

Corcyre

Nico

Tunis

Messine

Reggio

Cephalonie

brie

RIKIAH

Aschyr

Kairoan

Hammamet

Syracuse

MEDI

Mahadia

Petite Syrte

Serres

Arcadiople

Thessalonique

Thessalie

Bérée

Larisse

Rodosto

Eubée

Lesbos

HELLADE

Pergame

SERVIE

Naiss
Nissa

Butrinto

Danube

Tem

Pelr

Nicée

Pruse

ASIE

CONSTA

EMPIRE

Dijon  Champ du Mensonge  Bohème  Tch

Chalons  Bâle  Danube Fl.  Ratisbonne

GERMANIE

St. Gall  Constance  Augsbourg  Passau

Lyon  Coire  Bavière  Linz

Vienne  Salzbourg  Oster Reich

Yorée  Milan  Carinthie  Autriche

Turin  Pavie  Frioul  Esclavonie

Avignon  Padoue  Aquilée

Arles  Gênes  Parme  Venise

Provence  Florence  Ravenne

Aix  Toscane  Pentapole

Corse  Ancône  Jadera Zara

Spolète  Bos

Aleria  Spalatro

Sardaigne  ROME  Dalmatie

Mt. Cassin  Raguse

Bénévent  Bénévent Pte

Cagliari  Naples  Bari

Salerne Pte  Dyrrachi

Tarente

Otrante

Bizerte  Palerme  Calabre  Corcyre

Tunis  Sicile  Nicopo

MED

Reggio  Cephalonie

Hammamet  Messine  Zante

Mahadia  Syracuse  PÉLO

# ITALY
## COCKTAILS

### AN ELEGANT COLLECTION OF OVER 100 RECIPES INSPIRED BY ITALIA

## PAUL FEINSTEIN

CIDER MILL
PRESS

BOOK
PUBLISHERS

# ITALY COCKTAILS

ISBN-13: 978-1-64643-448-0
ISBN-10: 1-64643-448-X

This book may be ordered by mail from the publisher. Please include $5.99 for postage and handling. Please support your local bookseller first!

Books published by Cider Mill Press Book Publishers are available at special discounts for bulk purchases in the United States by corporations, institutions, and other organizations. For more information, please contact the publisher.

Cider Mill Press Book Publishers
"Where good books are ready for press"
501 Nelson Place
Nashville, Tennessee 37214
cidermillpress.com

Typography: Fino Sans, Avenir, Copperplate, Sackers, Warnock

Photography credits on page 410

Printed in India

23 24 25 26 27 REP 5 4 3 2 1

First Edition

# CONTENTS

# INTRODUCTION:

# A HISTORY OF ITALIAN COCKTAILS

When I first sat down to research and write this book, I was asked by several people how I would even come close to finding 100+ Italian cocktail recipes. It's a fair question; most people don't think of Italy as a cradle of original cocktail creations.

Sure, the average person probably knows about the Negroni, the Spritz, the Bellini, maybe the Americano, and maybe the more recently en vogue Negroni Sbagliato. But what they may not realize is that, without the contribution of Italy and Italian ingredients, there's practically no global cocktail scene at all.

Think about your Martini (you need vermouth), your Manhattan (same thing), the Boulevardier (vermouth and amaro), the Amaretto Sour (Italian amaretto), the Aviation (maraschino liqueur—Italian), Hanky Panky (Fernet-Branca and vermouth), the Last Word (maraschino liqueur), and the list goes on.

## ITALIAN COCKTAIL INGREDIENTS YOU MAY ALREADY KNOW

Italian ingredients include amaro, vermouth, bitters like Campari, aperitivos like Aperol and Select, fernet, grappa, limoncello, sambuca, prosecco, and many others. Galliano? Italian. Frangelico? Italian.

The ironic thing about Italy's grand tradition of cocktail ingredients is that they were used in places like New York and London for their cocktail scenes long before Italy adopted them for cocktail making at home. That quirk has a lot to do with the regionality of Italy, but also a slew of traditions that can be traced from Ancient Rome to about 2010, which is when Italy's classic cocktail culture started to truly catch up with the rest of the advanced cocktail drinking world— and even surpass it in many instances.

So, if you want to talk about Italian cocktails, and getting to 100+ recipes, we have to start at the beginning in Ancient Rome.

## THE ERAS OF ITALIAN COCKTAILS

Italian cocktail expert and historian Livio Lauro has a bird's-eye view of the history of Italian cocktails, and he breaks it up into eras. "There's the Archaic Era, the Vermouth Era, the Cocktail Era, the Disco Era, and the Modern Cocktail Era."

## THE ARCHAIC ERA

Lauro explains that if you go back to Ancient Rome, as far back as the second century B.C.E., you can find Roman elites consuming wines that were mixed with honey or mead. This marks the birth of aperitivo (see page 86), where Romans consumed these drinks as a prelude to meals, and to kick-start their appetites. If you want to get technical, this mixing of ingredients is one of the earliest forms of cocktail making.

If you fast forward a thousand years or so, Italy's relationship with cocktails stays pretty much the same, however Italy comes to the forefront of medicinal-based beverages. Lauro explains that, "between 900 to 1200 C.E., even to the 1400s, we have the University of Salerno that is on the cutting edge for the creation of and the studies of medicinal-based beverages, which ended up being in a lot of the recipes that we're drinking today."

When Lauro talks about medicinal-based beverages, he's really talking about alcoholic beverages that were mixed with botanicals that were believed to help people with any number of ailments—headaches, stomach issues, digestion, and so forth. The byproduct was also a nice buzz.

# THE VERMOUTH ERA

From there, we go to the late eighteenth century, where Italians became more enamored with bitters and with combining bitters and herbs with wine. This is what Lauro labels the Vermouth Era. Starting in 1786, Antonio Benedetto Carpano is credited with inventing the formula which ultimately would be referred to as vermouth. Carpano had a wine shop where people would gather and drink—not totally unlike the Romans in the Archaic Era, but this was more for the man on the street as opposed to elite social gatherings.

The late 1700s and into the 1800s in Italy is also when you see many major Italian brands begin to pop up. Nardini Grappa is founded in 1779. Luxardo in 1821. Fernet-Branca in 1845. Luigi Manzi creates Sambuca in 1850. Campari and Liquore Strega are invented in 1860. Martini & Rossi in 1863. Amaro Montenegro in 1885.

But the majority of these products were being shipped to other countries to be used in cocktails. In Italy, these products were regional, mostly being sipped neat as aperitifs or digestifs.

In 1848, Italian Unification put all the regions of Italy under one roof. According to cocktail historian David Wondrich, this started to change Italy's drinking culture as well. "In the late nineteenth century, Italy is unified, and there's tourism, and you're beginning to see American-style bars inside of big Italian hotels. One of the things Italians noticed was that Americans liked putting bitters into vermouth, and the Italians had a lot of bitters. They were probably already doing this,

but it gave [the custom] a huge boost. The Americano comes out of that in the 1880s and 1890s and they were putting it on ice, with soda, etc. And it's not just Campari, it was any bitter and any vermouth."

Wondrich explains that the first real Italian cocktail to get traction outside of Italy, making it to Paris and to London in the 1880s or 1890s, was Fernet-Branca with vermouth. At the same time, aperitivo culture was starting to take different shapes and forms in different regions of Italy, where drinks like Campari with vermouth and soda, the Milano-Torino, and bottled aperitivos were becoming more popular as pre-dinner aperitifs.

# THE COCKTAIL ERA AND
# THE DISCO ERA

From the Vermouth Era, we get to the turn of the twentieth century and Italy's first real cocktail era. However, this era can be subdivided into three periods. As Lauro says, "There's the Italian one, which has drinks like Campari with vermouth and soda, and the Americano. Then, there's the American Bar movement where American prohibition is driving cocktailing in other countries. Places like Paris are adopting the American style of making drinks, and Italians are starting to compete with that thinking, especially in high-end hotels in major Italian cities. And then there's Futurism."

Futurism was an Italian cultural movement that gained notoriety in the 1920s and 1930s for its adoption of new technology, a complete rejection of anything that wasn't Italian, and a desire to remake or rethink everything in Italian society—including cocktails. (They also played footsie with the Fascists, so they have that going against them.)

In the first few decades of the twentieth Century, you see Italy beginning to create its own cocktails (Negroni in 1919), establishing a pre-dinner drinking culture that's similar to today (Spritzes in the early 1920s), and becoming much more proficient in making American-style cocktails, and you have the Futurists trying to tread their own path of artistic, anti-globalist, anarchic drink-making.

World War II nearly wiped out every major Italian booze company. Distillers that had factories near ports were bombed and destroyed. But after the war ended, there was a new Italian renaissance. An economic boom happened in Italy in the 1950s and 1960s, which ushered in a whole new way of thinking about cocktails.

Hollywood celebrities played a part in this, and so did the 1960 Federico Fellini film *La Dolce Vita* ("the sweet life"), which epitomized the idea that Italy was a place for people to come and drink well, eat well, and bask in the Italian lifestyle. American tourism took off at this time, and the hotel bars in Rome, Milan, and Venice were hot spots for a who's-who crowd and their moneyed hangers-on.

But that leads to the next era, the era of disco, which Lauro proclaims was the Dark Ages of Italian cocktailing. The Disco Era postdates the American disco craze by almost ten years, and the 1980s were a time where thousands of students and young Italians flocked to Italian *discotecas*, with their disco balls and sweet, multicolored drinks. This extends through the era of cocktail flair, where bartenders mimicked Tom Cruise from the movie *Cocktail*, and incorporated elaborate bottle flipping and circus-like acts into a bartending show.

In the early 2000s, while serious mixology started to take off around the world in every major metropolis, Italy remained stuck in the past, with its *Cocktail* flair. However, Italian bartenders were working at some of the most important bars in London, New York, Paris, and other major cultural centers. These bartenders were not only getting schooled on true classic cocktailing, but also on how to incorporate homemade syrups, on how to use market-fresh ingredients, and on how cocktailing could become a true profession.

# THE MODERN COCKTAIL ERA

The real inflection point for Italy as a modern cocktail country comes in 2010, what Lauro refers to as the Modern Cocktail Era. Around that time, four Italian bartenders started the Jerry Thomas Project (see page 32), one of the first Italian speakeasies, along with a bartending school to train Italians on the fundamentals of making classic cocktails, following the recipes of famed bartender Jerry Thomas. The project started slowly, but in a few years, Italy's cocktail culture began to swing in their direction. Their disciples opened their own bars, Italian bartenders started to come back from abroad and open their own establishments, and a movement kicked off, returning to a time when bartending was taken seriously, and aiming to remake the future of bartending in Italy.

But if there's one throughline that connects every aspect of drinking in Italy, it's food. Italians drink to eat and eat to drink. It's part of the culture, it's part of the ritual, it's a way to get a night started, and it's a way to wind things down. More and more, cocktails are even being paired with dinner in the same way wine has been.

Today, in Italy, you now have a robust cocktail culture. In every major city (and now in nearly every smaller city and town), you can find serious mixologists making drinks at the highest levels. Italian ingredients have never been more popular, and the newest trend streaming through this highly skilled bartending community is to make their own products. You can now find multiple Italian gin companies, new-age vermouths, unique aperitivo liqueurs, and more. Bartenders are using advanced techniques to infuse spirits, clarify alcohols, create homemade syrups, and concoct bitters. Italy's long heritage of creating the best cocktail ingredients in the world has entered a new phase, and the bars and bartenders of Italy are finally in lockstep with their past.

*Cin cin. Salute. Alla tua. Cent'anni!*
—Paul Feinstein

# HOW TO DRINK

# LIKE AN ITALIAN

# FRESH MATTERS

In Italy, everything is regional, and everything is seasonal. Every part of the country has different traditions and cultural quirks, but if there's one thing that all Italians can agree on, it's that fresh is best. That means Italian cocktail menus typically follow the seasons since most of their fresh fruit mixers and garnishes are dependent on the crops available at the moment.

# FOOD AND DRINK

Everything in Italy is tied into food. Coffee goes with *cornetti* (pastries) in the morning. Lunch hovers around 12:30 p.m. and 1 p.m. followed by a break and a mini-aperitivo (depending on your region). That aperitivo consists of low-ABV drinks and salty snacks. Work usually recommences at 4 p.m. and goes until about 7 p.m. where there's a second aperitivo—more low-ABV cocktails (Spritzes, Negronis, etc.) with chips, peanuts, taralli, or sometimes small buffets. Dinner, 8 p.m. and later, goes with wine and more recently, cleverly paired cocktails. After dinner comes dessert, followed by coffee, followed by digestivo, which contains more low-ABV drinks to settle you down.

# APERITIVO

The tradition of aperitivo goes back to Ancient Rome, but today, it's generally a pre-dinner social hour or two where you can drink and snack, hang out on the piazza, and mingle with new friends. Some of these happy hour–esque times include free buffets, but it's generally not a great idea to fill up before dinner. No matter; the aperitivo food and drinks serve a larger purpose, and it's to get your stomach prepared for dinner.

# DIGESTIVO

After dinner there's dessert and coffee. But after that, there's digestivo. Traditionally, this is a time where Italians will sip on amari, fernets, grappe, and other bitter liqueurs to help settle their stomachs and wind down for the night. More recently, bartenders have been exploring this category and time with more intricate versions depending on whether you want to end the night there or keep it going much later (looking at you, Espresso Martini).

## DRINK, BUT NOT TO GET DRUNK

Italians love their alcohol and their extensive heritage is tied to an unbelievable number of liqueurs and wines. But drinking is always done with food, meant to stimulate, meant to digest, and meant to enhance. Of course, getting drunk is sometimes a byproduct of all of this, but that's not necessarily the aim. You'll find the history of Italy's cocktail culture to be laced with mostly low-ABV drinks, though that has changed dramatically since 2010.

## KNOW YOUR REGION AND KNOW YOUR LIQUEURS

Italy has a range of homegrown products unrivaled by any other country. Each region has its own version of amaro, while at the same time there are regions specializing in specific products like vermouth in Torino, grappa in Friuli, sambuca in Marche, Strega in Campania, aperitivo (the liqueur) in Veneto, and so on. These names will all mean more to you as you read this book, but for now just know that regions matter. You wouldn't say that California is the same as Alabama just because they're both in the United States—it's no different in Italy.

# BITTER IS BETTER

The Italian palate is fairly advanced when it comes to bitter flavors and the cocktails reflect this down the line. Bitter herbs are ubiquitous in Italian liqueurs, and the profiles can range from slightly sweet to an "Is this poison?" level of bitterness.

# THE ITALIAN COCKTAIL WORLD IS RAPIDLY CHANGING

The cocktail revolution began around 2010 in Italy, where incredibly respectable bars started popping up in major cities with major league cocktail programs. This is mostly thanks to the Jerry Thomas Project (see page 32), which spread top-flight cocktail bars from the confines of five-star hotels to city streets throughout Italy. Today, you can find stellar cocktail programs, run by bartenders who have trained at some of the best spots around the world, even in smaller cities. Italy is no longer a second-rate country for cocktails, and with the best products already made here, it's just getting better and better.

# HOW TO STOCK THE PERFECT ITALIAN BAR CART

If you want to drink like an Italian at home, and if you want to be able to make the cocktails in this book, you're going to need to stock up on a bevy of Italian products. But start slowly, because the exercise of turning your house into an Italian cocktail haven can start to get pricy.

## TOOLS FOR SERVING DRINKS

**BAR CART:** If you want to impress your guests, and really get into the theme of this book, find yourself a vintage Italian bar cart. These carts are usually trolley style, meant for bringing tableside at an Italian restaurant. They typically have two shelves, as well, to fit all the different types of Italian bottles.

## TOOLS FOR MAKING DRINKS

**COCKTAIL SHAKER:** You'll need this to make virtually every recipe in this book. The cocktail shaker is the most crucial tool for chilling a drink, frothing a drink, and simply infusing flavors together.

**MIXING GLASS:** A large pint glass, essentially, that can handle the rigor of stirring and shaking.

**STRAINERS:** There's the standard strainer that comes with a mixing glass, there's a fine mesh strainer for really ensuring no solid bits make it into your drink, and a cheesecloth for the ultimate strain without any chance of solids.

BARSPOON: Used to mix drinks and also a unit of measurement in some recipes.

JIGGER: To be as precise as possible with your pours, a jigger is a great way to ensure accuracy.

MUDDLER: For smashing fruits and herbs into the tiniest of bits to release their juices, oils, and aromas.

COCKTAIL PICKS/STIRRERS: For piercing those olives, oranges, and lemons. For this book, I use a chic set of picks and drink stirrers from Love & Victory.

# GLASSWARE TERMINOLOGY

I recommend starting with chic Italian brands like Atelier Crestani for fine art pieces or Bormioli for something more functional. For avant-garde pieces, check out Mamo glassware. Other brands I use and that are featured in this book include Nick & Nora glasses from Chef&Sommelier, etched rocks glasses from Love & Victory, and more finery from SIR/MADAM.

In this book you'll need old-fashioned/rocks glasses, Nick & Nora glasses, coupes, Collins/highball glasses, and martini glasses.

# SPIRITS AND LIQUEURS

If you want to truly stock an Italian bar cart with the proper Italian bottles, there's a lot to choose from. And if you want to make most of the drinks in this book, you'll need these at home. From the good people at Eataly, here's a general suggestion broken up by region:

**Piemonte**—Cocchi/Barolo Chinato

**Piemonte**—Romano Levi Grappa

**Lombardia**—Braulio Amaro

**Trentino-Alto Adige**—Cappelletti Aperitivo

**Friuli**—Nonino Grappa

**Toscana**—Galliano

**Marche**—Amaro Dell'Erborista

**Marche**—Meletti Sambuca

**Sardegna**—Silvio Carta Mirto

**Abruzzo**—Campari

**Abruzzo**—Aperol

**Lazio**—Paolucci Amaro Ciociaro

**Campania**—Liquore Strega

**Basilicata**—Amaro Lucano

**Sicilia**—Vulcanica Vodka

**Calabria**—Vecchio Amaro Del Capo

To add to this list, you'll also want the following:

**VERMOUTH**: Martini & Rossi, Baldoria, Cocchi, Carpano

**BITTERS**: Luxardo, Cappelletti, Select Aperitivo, Contratto Bitter

**PROSECCO**: Cinzano, Martini & Rossi

**GIN**: Malfy, Engine Gin, Gin Dall'Olio, London Dry

**WHISKEY**: Busker, Ardbeg, Michter's, Glen Grant, Angel's Envy Bourbon

**RUM**: Arrangè

**TEQUILA AND MEZCAL**: Casamigos, Espolón, Don Julio 1942, Espadin, Yola

**LIQUEURS**: Fernet-Branca, Disaronno, Italicus, Averna, Cynar, Frangelico, Poli, Marolo, Pallini

**BRANDY**: Vecchia Romagna

## MIXERS

**FRUIT**: Have plenty of oranges, lemons, limes, and grapefruits on hand, but you'll also need everything from strawberries and grapes to pears, cherries, and olives.

**HERBS**: Stock up on mint, thyme, rosemary, and basil to start.

**SYRUPS**: There are a lot of different types of syrups in this book. Many of the recipes have homemade versions, though you can find bottled ones at most specialty liquor stores.

**BITTERS**: Angostura is the most prevalent in this book, but there are many others with different infused flavors.

**BALSAMIC VINEGAR:** That's right, balsamic vinegar. There are some excellent recipes in this book from both Giusti (see page 360) and Ponti (see page 402)—two of the most well-known vinegar brands in the world.

**CARBONATED MIXERS:** You'll want plenty of soda water, tonic, ginger ale, and other sweetened and unsweetened carbonated beverages for mixing a variety of drinks.

**SALINE SOLUTION:** A mix of salt and water, saline solution can be used to enhance or balance flavors. To make it, use 1/4 cup of salt and 1 cup of water, mix in a saucepan over heat until fully dissolved. Allow to cool and pour into a dropper bottle.

# TECHNIQUES

**SHAKE:** Shake will refer to shaking a drink with a metal cocktail shaker. It's nearly always with ice, but there are many recipes that call for a dry shake with no ice.

**STRAIN:** Straining is the process of pouring your shaken-up mixer through a strainer of some kind to get rid of hard bits in the cocktail.

**STIR:** Fairly self-explanatory, but the amount you stir, how vigorously, and for how long will be spelled out in the recipes.

**OTHER:** Throughout the book, there will be recipes that talk about making syrups, shrubs, infusions, and more. The specific instructions for each of these advanced homemade techniques will be spelled out in the recipes. Most if not all of these can be purchased at specialty stores—but if you want to bartend like an Italian, you'll make them at home.

# THE ITALIAN COCKTAIL CLASSICS:

# NEGRONIS, AMERICANOS & SPRITZES

CAMPARI NEGRONI

AMERICANO

VECCHIO STILE (OLD FASHIONED) JTP

IMPROVED AVIATION

MANHATTAN JTP

SELECT SPRITZ

MILANO-TORINO

BELLINI

MONTGOMERY

NEGRONI SBAGLIATO

ROSSINI

GARIBALDI

HUGO

IL CARDINALE

NEGRONI FLEUR DE LYS

NEG-MEX

IL BOMBARDINO (THE BOMB)

BOULEVARDIER

THE GODFATHER

DECISONE

IL RIGENERATORE (THE REGENERATOR)

COPPA DI BRIVIDI (GLASS OF SHIVERS)

What is considered a classic Italian cocktail? I'm sure what immediately comes to mind is the Negroni or Spritz, or maybe the Bellini and Americano. And yes, these all belong to the classic Italian cocktail canon that has helped revolutionize cocktailing around the world.

But there's much more to this history than these celebrated drinks. You could argue that any classic cocktail made with vermouth should be considered Italian—think Martinis and Manhattans. You could argue that the Aviation, Montgomery, and Godfather should all be considered Italian.

The fact of the matter is, without Italian ingredients—bitters like Campari, vermouth, prosecco, aperitivos, and many others—this list of classic cocktails would look a lot smaller.

The following recipes are a collection of the indelible drinks either made in Italy or using Italian ingredients with long histories. You'll also find a section on Futurist cocktails (see page 79), that have their own fascinating 100-year history that was almost entirely forgotten.

# CAMPARI NEGRONI

CAMPARI
VIA SACCHETTI, 20
20099 SESTO SAN GIOVANNI MILANO MI, ITALY

The king of all Italian cocktails, the Negroni was first created around 1919 by bartender Fosco Scarselli at Café Casoni in Florence. The story goes that a man, Count Camillo Negroni, would ask Scarselli to strengthen his classic Americano by removing the soda water and adding gin. Scarselli obliged, adding an orange slice as the topper, and the Negroni came into being. More than 100 years later, the equal-parts drink of gin, red vermouth, and Campari has spawned dozens of variations, including many in this book, but the original still holds the crown for the greatest Italian cocktail, and very little is going to change that.

---

✳

**GLASSWARE:** Old-fashioned glass
**GARNISH:** Half an orange wheel

---

- 1 oz. Campari
- 1 oz. Bulldog Gin
- 1 oz. 1757 Vermouth di Torino Rosso

1. Fill an old-fashioned glass with ice.

2. Add all the ingredients and stir.

3. Garnish with an orange wheel.

# AMERICANO

The Americano was first served in the late 1860s at Gaspare Campari's Caffè Campari, where it was originally called the Milano-Torino, due to Campari being from Milan and the vermouth from Torino. The Americano name (which means "American-style") is a nod to how Americans would drink vermouth by adding some bitters and making it a Vermouth Cocktail. It wasn't until a couple decades later that the addition of soda water made its way into the official recipe. No matter what you call it, the combo of Campari, vermouth, and soda is refreshing, bitter, and a tad sweet in all the right ways. It's a lovely aperitif and is incredibly easy to make.

✳

**GLASSWARE: Rocks glass**

**GARNISH: Orange slice and/or lemon peel**

- 1 oz. Campari
- 1 oz. 1757 Vermouth di Torino
- Soda water, to top

1. Fill a rocks glass with ice.

2. Add Campari and vermouth and stir.

3. Top with a splash of soda.

4. Garnish with an orange slice and lemon peel.

# THE JERRY THOMAS SPEAKEASY

## VICOLO CELLINI, 30, 00186 ROMA RM, ITALY

You could argue that the Jerry Thomas Speakeasy is the most important bar in Italy in terms of shaping the modern cocktail scene. Opened in 2010 by bartenders Leonardo Leuci, Antonio Parlapiano, Roberto Artusio, and Alessandro Procoli, the Jerry, as it's affectionately known, was created to bring Italy's cocktail culture into the twenty-first century while simultaneously recalling the nineteenth century.

What that meant was scouring the recipes of the legendary bartender Jerry Thomas, recreating his drinks, and then taking those drinks into all-new dimensions. The team also wanted to uproot Italy's traditionalist attitudes towards drinking—mainly that drinking was limited to pre-dinner aperitivos consisting of low-ABV cocktails, wine with dinner, and post-dinner low-ABV digestivos, which mostly meant drinking amari, Strega, Fernet-Branca, and other liqueurs, neat or on the rocks.

Owners Alessandro Procoli, Roberto Artusio,
Antonio Parlapiano, and Leonardo Leuci

The Jerry Thomas crew also felt that Italy was stuck in the 1980s, when flipping bottles was en vogue and the methods governed by the International Bartenders Association (IBA) were sacrosanct. And they wanted to take a sledgehammer to all of it.

Little did the team know that they would create a tidal wave of modern and classic cocktailing that would ripple throughout the entire country and begin a whole new way for Italians to think about the world of mixology outside of fancy five-star hotels that were mostly geared to tourists.

The bar also helped put Italy on the global map, inspiring Italian bartenders to ditch cushy jobs in London and New York and come back to Italy to open their own bars. The accolades have come in as Jerry Thomas and multiple other Italian establishments now find themselves perpetually on the World's 50 Best Bars list.

***Let's begin with how you [Leonardo Leuci] got started in bartending, and then how it led to the Jerry Thomas Project.***

The Jerry Thomas project is composed of four people. All of us started bartending between twenty and twenty-five years ago, and all of us have international experience. For me, I was working a lot in the Caribbean for seven or eight years, as well as in France, Turkey, and Morocco. Roberto [Artusio] was working in London and Copenhagen, and Alessandro [Procoli] was in New York. Everything started a little bit as a joke. In 2009, we had a sort of reunion because I was coming back from Turks and Caicos and Alessandro was coming back from New York. It had been five or six years since we had chatted or had a beer, so we decided to get together and we started to talk about what's going on in Italy, and nothing was happening.

In 2009, Italy was stuck in this flair era, like the TGI Friday's influence that was almost dead all around the world. But it was still strong in Italy and there were only two big influences on the market at that time—these flair things, and the old IBA standard that was being revived in hotel bars. But all of us, looking from a different perspective, understood that all around the world something else was happening. There was a new golden age of cocktails arriving. People started to be interested in seriously rediscovering what's happening, like in the Prohibition era. David Wondrich's book *Imbibe* had arrived on the market and changed the point of view about everything, but in Italy, nobody noticed. So, we were the first group of people that decided to take everything that was happening around the world and bring it to Italy.

**How long did it take for people to adopt what you were doing? Because you were teaching all these bartenders, and these bartenders were then going off and starting their own bars in Italy, right?**

Totally. But in the first couple of years, people were saying, "We don't want any change," like the IBA people and the flair people who accused us of essentially downgrading the level of Italian mixology. Because we started to introduce, for example, the jigger, and nobody was using the jigger, so we started to teach people. Look, anyone can make a Manhattan, anyone can pour a Manhattan, it's simple, it's easy, and everybody can do a Manhattan with free pouring. But if you want to make "that" Manhattan that is in "that" book, with "that" recipe, you have to be really careful on what you are pouring. That takes into account the product you're pouring. If you want to reproduce a cocktail from 1860, you have to know that when it's gin in the recipe it's genever [a malty Dutch precursor to gin] in reality. You have to know when you say Jamaican rum that it's not talking about a cheap Jamaican rum that you can find in the supermarket. So, all these small details we started to introduce to the market and a lot of people started to really hate what we were doing.

The impact of Jerry Thomas was very big and a lot of other people wanted to open speakeasies. We also had a big influence on what some companies started to import in Italy. The genever market for example, there was not one imported genever in Italy and now you can find thirty-five different ones. Genever was our most important spirit at the time because we really wanted to replicate Jerry Thomas.

**How did it feel to see all these other bars start to pop up since you were the ones teaching these people in Italy?**

It felt great. But we didn't stop there. Every year we keep bringing very important people from all around the world. And you have to imagine that the second time we brought David Wondrich and Jeff Berry to Italy, we had to rent a theater with a couple thousand seats for the people who just wanted to follow that seminar. It was crazy, and we started to do these all around Italy. After a couple of years, we started to be invited all around Europe because our project was not only to rediscover forgotten cocktails, but it was also kind of a way of life. It was dressing a certain way, and acting a certain way; it was a bit hipster what we were doing. But ultimately it was about focusing on the importance of what a bartender was in the past, because in my mind what bartenders had lost was that seniority they had in the past. We wanted to bring back the seniority of bartenders in the community. And we also wanted to make sure to bring back the idea that a bar is a social place, and a place where you go because it's where you want to meet people.

***Have you seen the local cocktail drinking culture change? Are you seeing people change their drinking behavior?***

Absolutely, yes. We don't have one bar, we have three bars in Rome. The requests of people are really changing a lot. Now, the Negroni is a standard, the Gin & Tonic is becoming like a comfort drink. Ten years ago, it wasn't like that; vodka tonic was the standard comfort drink. Nobody was asking for a Negroni. Now the Negroni is really strong and is one of the best-selling drinks at Jerry Thomas. The Spritz is the fastest growing drink everywhere.

Another big thing that we have done that I think is unique is that we created a brand that is called Del Professore, a vermouth brand that we sold to Campari. This brand is what really drove the vermouth renaissance in Europe over the past ten years because we were the first producer to reintroduce an artisanal production of vermouth in 150 years. I remember when we started the project in 2010 and I started to talk about the importance of vermouth in the history of mixology, people were looking at me like I was a crazy man. Most of the people who were making classic drinks like Manhattans were doing the IBA recipe where the vermouth was just a splash. But when we started to reproduce the 1888 Manhattan where it's half and half, or in the beginning of the 1900s when the Martini was made with Italian vermouth and fifty percent with gin. So, we let people understand that if you want to replicate these kinds of recipes, vermouth is very important. This is a well-balanced drink where vermouth has a really strong impact, so it has to be good.

# VECCHIO STILE (OLD FASHIONED) JTP

JERRY THOMAS SPEAKEASY
VICOLO CELLINI, 30, 00186 ROMA RM, ITALY

The Jerry Thomas team is known for improving upon classic cocktails, and the Vecchio Stile is no exception. Vecchio Stile is the Italian way to say Old Fashioned, and this version of the drink incorporates lots of the old with plenty of the new. The most interesting variations would be the dashes of bergamot and chocolate bitters in addition to the Rum Arrangè, which is a rum infused with fruits and spices. This cocktail will fascinate and surprise Old Fashioned fans and if you're one of them, you might think twice before making one the "old fashioned" way.

**GLASSWARE:** Old-fashioned glass

**GARNISH:** Lemon zest, orange zest

- 1 sugar cube
- 3 dashes chocolate bitters
- 3 dashes bergamot bitters
- Splash of water
- 2 oz. bourbon
- ½ oz. Rum Arrangè

1. Add the sugar cube, two bitters, and splash of water to an old-fashioned glass and muddle.

2. Add the rest of the ingredients, fill the glass with ice, and stir for about 20 seconds.

3. Garnish with lemon and orange zest.

# IMPROVED AVIATION

JERRY THOMAS SPEAKEASY
VICOLO CELLINI, 30, 00186 ROMA RM, ITALY

The original Aviation cocktail has a mix of gin, lemon juice, maraschino liqueur, and crème de violette. Antonio "Il Professore" Parlapiano of the Jerry Thomas team wanted to improve upon this early-twentieth-century gem and did so by switching out the lemon for lime and the maraschino liqueur for lavender syrup. The result is a tangy cocktail with a touch of floral sweetness, and a hint of bitterness.

**GLASSWARE:** Coupette

**GARNISH:** Lemon zest, 1 small dried rose

- 1 ⅔ oz. London Dry Gin
- 4/5 oz. lavender syrup
- 1/6 oz. violet liqueur

- 1 oz. lime juice
- 2 dashes wild rose bitters

1. Add all the ingredients to a shaker with ice and shake vigorously for 10 seconds.

2. Strain the cocktail into a coupette.

3. Garnish with lemon zest and a little dried rose.

# MANHATTAN JTP

JERRY THOMAS SPEAKEASY
VICOLO CELLINI, 30, 00186 ROMA RM, ITALY

While the team at the Jerry Thomas Speakeasy adheres to the classics of cocktailing, they always seem to find room to make the drinks their own. That's especially true for this iteration of a Manhattan. The most sizable change is in the use of Creole bitters—while it's only a few drops, you'll feel the kicks of cayenne and pink peppercorn adding a new dimension to the drink. Additionally, the curaçao brings in an orange flavor typically reserved for the drink's garnish. This sophisticated cocktail reaches a whole new level and will impress any Manhattan aficionado with its fun and surprising twists.

**GLASSWARE:** Coupette

- 1 ½ oz. rye whiskey
- 1 oz. red vermouth
- ⅓ oz. Del Professore Vermouth Chinato
- 1/10 oz. curaçao
- 3 drops Creole bitters
- Lemon zest, for spraying the glass

1. Add all the ingredients, except for the lemon zest, to a mixing glass.

2. Add ice until it covers the surface of the mixture and stir.

3. Strain the cocktail into a coupette.

4. Spray the edge of the glass with the essential oils of a lemon zest.

# CAMPARINO IN GALLERIA

## P.ZA DEL DUOMO, 21, 20121 MILANO MI, ITALY

In 1867, Campari opened its first bar, Caffè Campari, around the corner from the famous Duomo. In 1915, Gaspare Campari's son Davide opened a sister bar, Camparino, which quickly became a Milan institution for any number of local and international luminaries.

Today, Camparino in Galleria symbolizes aperitivo culture in Milan and is divided into two bars: Bar di Passo on the ground floor, which is like walking back into 1915 and specializes in classic cocktails, and Sala Spiritello on the second floor, which leans into innovative mixology.

The head bartender at Camparino is Tommaso Cecca, who fell in love with the brand early in his life and leapt at the opportunity to run Camparino when it came.

### What about Milan inspires you?

Milan is a magical city, full of heritage mixed with innovation, a source of inspiration. "Aperitivo" culture binds intrinsically to the city's DNA. The customers' lifestyle and habits help shape and fuel my creativity, guiding me to bring excellent-quality cocktails to the bar that perfectly reflect the context in which I work, which is Milan. It is no coincidence that Campari bitter was born here.

### What do you think makes Camparino unique?

It has become a landmark for those who are passionate about mixology, considering that we have gained a great boost of recognition from entering the most prestigious ranks in the field: the World's 50 Best Bars. Another distinct point is our look and service style: nothing is left to chance, from the white jackets to the perfect serve of classic Campari cocktails, in complete harmony with the place in which we have the honor to work.

### Do you think about the history of Italian cocktails, and try to incorporate any of that history into your bartending?

Absolutely. In my humble opinion, if the U.S. pioneered the culture of cocktails since the late 1800s, Italy played a key role in the 1900s. Just think about Count Camillo Negroni: it is thanks to him that the most-imbibed cocktail came alive. More than 100 years ago, he was already sipping the cocktail that is now one of the best known in the world.

# SELECT SPRITZ

SELECT
VENICE

The most iconic drink in the Select portfolio, the Select Spritz is also commonly known as the Venetian Spritz. Select Aperitivo was created in 1920 in Venice and the company claims to have started the trend of drinking this classic liqueur with soda water and prosecco. Regardless of who initiated the Spritz trend (as of this writing it's one of the most popular drinks in the world), we're all better for it. The Select version is more complex and more bitter than its rivals and is perfect for the pre-dinner ritual of drinking with friends in the summer.

**GLASSWARE:** White wine glass

**GARNISH:** Large Castelvetrano olive

- 3 oz. chilled prosecco
- 2 oz. Select Aperitivo
- 1 oz. soda water

1. Fill a white wine glass with ice.

2. Add the prosecco then the Select Aperitivo and soda water and stir gently.

3. Garnish with an olive.

# MILANO-TORINO

CAMPARINO IN GALLERIA
P.ZA DEL DUOMO, 21, 20121 MILANO MI, ITALY

**D**epending on where you're from or where the person you're asking is from, this cocktail can be called the Milano-Torino or the Torino-Milano. That's because its two components are Campari from Milan and vermouth from Turin. The first Milano-Torino ever served was in Gaspare Campari's Caffè Campari in the 1860s. This classic cocktail is similar to the Americano, but doesn't use soda water to add carbonation. The drink is bittersweet and simple.

✳

**GLASSWARE:** Rocks glass

**GARNISH:** Orange slice

- 1 ½ oz. Campari
- 1 ½ oz. 1757 Vermouth di Torino

1. Fill a rocks glass with ice.

2. Add Campari and vermouth to a mixing glass with ice and stir.

3. Strain the cocktail into a rocks glass.

4. Garnish with an orange slice.

# HARRY'S BAR

The Cipriani name should mean something to you. Maybe you've stayed in a Cipriani hotel or eaten at a Cipriani restaurant. But none of that would exist without the first and most important property in the entire Cipriani story: Harry's Bar.

The story goes that in the 1920s, Giuseppe Cipriani helped out a young American named Harry Pickering who had been left stranded in Venice. Cipriani gave Pickering some money and helped him find his way back home. Karma does in fact exist, because in 1931, Pickering came back to Venice to repay his debt and asked Cipriani to open a bar with him in the city. Cipriani agreed and proclaimed that they would call it Harry's Bar.

Harry's itself is small, simple, and refined, but its reputation is larger than life. Not only is it the home of the Bellini, but it also has some claims on other famous cocktails like the Rossini (disputed on page 54), the Stinger, and the Montgomery—a cocktail that was invented at Harry's by Ernest Hemingway (see page 53).

Over the years, Harry's Bar has seen its fair share of famous patrons including Charlie Chaplin, Orson Welles, Truman Capote, Peggy Guggenheim, Frank Lloyd Wright, and Joe DiMaggio. It's also featured in Hemingway's novel, *Across the River and into the Trees.*

Harry's is so singular a bar that in 2001, the Ministry of Cultural Heritage in Italy declared it a national monument. To this day, Harry's is one of the most beloved bars and restaurants in the world. It's still hosting famous guests, and it's still serving meticulously made cocktails for when the next Hemingway comes along to get inspired.

# BELLINI

HARRY'S BAR
CALLE VALLARESSO, 1323, 30124 VENEZIA VE, ITALY

Invented by Giuseppe Cipriani at Harry's Bar in Venice, Italy, in 1948, the Bellini is an all-time classic cocktail. Allegedly, the drink was named after Giovanni Bellini, whose pink-hued paintings helped inspire the creation. The key to any great Bellini, and in particular the original, is making sure you have the freshest ingredients. So, take a little extra time to make your own peach puree instead of buying it in a store. It's worth it.

---

✳

**GLASSWARE:** Collins glass

---

- **2 oz. White Peach Puree (see recipe)**

- **6 oz. Prosecco DOC or Conegliano Valdobbiadene Prosecco Superiore DOCG**

**1.** Strain the puree into a collins glass.

**2.** Add the prosecco and stir gently.

## WHITE PEACH PUREE

Wash two ripe white peaches and remove the pits. Using a potato masher (not a blender, as it adds too much air to the juice), mash the peaches along with their peels.

# MONTGOMERY

HARRY'S BAR
CALLE VALLARESSO, 1323, 30124 VENEZIA VE, ITALY

According to Harry's Bar lore the Montgomery is a version of a Dry Martini created by none other than Ernest Hemingway. Arrigo Cipriani (Giuseppe Cipriani's son) chronicled the history of the bar in *Harry's Bar Venezia, Le ricette della tradizione*, and said, "[Hemingway] preferred that the Vermouth, in respect to the Gin, not exceed a proportion of one to fifteen. The same proportion—Hemingway would say—with which the famous English General Montgomery was fighting his battles during the Second World War: fifteen of his soldiers against for each of his enemy's."

The cocktail served at Harry's Bar is a perfectly balanced and perfectly dry version of a Martini with exacting measurements to achieve the result. Prepare carefully or you won't be able to picture Hemingway drinking away the day beside the Venice canals, saluting to the great British general.

**GLASSWARE: Tumbler**
**GARNISH: Lemon rind (optional)**

- **3 oz. London Dry Gin**
- **1/5 oz. dry vermouth**

1. Chill the vermouth and gin, and a tumbler, in the freezer.

2. Pour the vermouth and gin into the tumbler and stir.

3. Garnish with a lemon rind (if you hate Hemingway and want to change the original recipe).

# BAR BASSO

Opened in 1947 by Mirko Stocchetto, Bar Basso has played a pivotal role in the cocktail culture of Milan. This is the home of the now uber-famous Negroni Sbagliato (see page 57). It's here that the Rossini was, allegedly, invented. And it's here that the concept of aperitivo, drinking low-ABV cocktails in a social way before dinner, really started to take shape.

Today, Bar Basso is run by Mirko's son Maurizio, and it still holds a place as one of the best bars in the world and home to classic and not-so-classic cocktails. Mirko allegedly invented hundreds of cocktails, and many of them are on full display inside this legendary spot.

I talked to Maurizio Stocchetto to get the real story behind the Negroni Sbagliato and more.

***Let's talk about the Negroni Sbagliato. It has become more famous recently and your father is the inventor of this drink. Can you talk a bit about its history and what you're seeing now?***

The Negroni Sbagliato has been around for more than fifty years. In the 1960s, cocktail bars were mostly like gentlemen's clubs. There were lots of men at the counter and the ladies were coming to the bar mostly with their husbands or with other people, but they were sitting at the tables. After 1968, and after counterculture, lots of ladies started to work. And sometimes it was controversial because the parents did not want to have young girls finding jobs. They wanted them to get married, they wanted them to keep studying and maybe become teachers, but not professionals. But then a lot of ladies started to do it, especially in Milano. So, we started to have a lot of ladies coming to the bar and ordering their own drinks.

My father is a Venetian, and he knew very well about the Bellini (see page 50), so he made another cocktail, the Rossini (see page 58), with sparkling champagne and strawberries. It was created at Bar Basso, not at Harry's Bar (see page 49). And he started to develop many cocktails using sparkling wine instead of primary spirits just to make it with a lower amount of alcohol. The Negroni Sbagliato was just another development of using sparkling wine in cocktails. My father was born in the 1930s and he loved Martinis and he loved the real Negroni, so he called the drink Sbagliato, which means "mistaken" in a kind of joking way. It was kind of ironic, because he had a limited view about this cocktail because it wasn't as powerful as a real Negroni. Most people say that he took the wrong bottle making a Negroni, but no bartender in those days would have made a Negroni using sparkling wine instead of gin unless it was on purpose. So, I think it's very ironic because my father was very creative and he developed many, many cocktails and anytime he was interviewed in magazines or anything, he would never mention the Sbagliato because it was kind of a joke. But after the 1990s it started to become popular. Sbagliato for us has always been a cocktail that even during hard times, it put us on the map. We have become very, very, hip and fashionable.

# NEGRONI SBAGLIATO

BAR BASSO
VIA PLINIO, 39, 20133 MILANO MI, ITALY

Although it's achieved a resurgence of fame (thanks to Emma D'Arcy's now viral interview), the Negroni Sbagliato came about in the late 1960s or early 1970s when Mirko Stocchetto of the famed Bar Basso in Milan poured it for the first time. The legend is that he made the drink by mistake when he accidentally poured prosecco instead of gin while making a Negroni. "Sbagliato" actually means "mistaken," so it would be a fitting name for this "accidental" creation. But according to Stocchetto's son Maurizio, the name was more tongue-in-cheek.

**GLASSWARE:** Old-fashioned glass (Atelier Crestani)

**GARNISH:** Orange slice

- 1 oz. Campari
- 1 oz. Cinzano Prosecco
- 1 oz. 1757 Vermouth di Torino Rosso

1. Fill an old-fashioned glass with ice.

2. Add all the ingredients and stir.

3. Garnish with a slice of orange.

# ROSSINI

BAR BASSO
VIA PLINIO, 39, 20133 MILANO MI, ITALY

There's debate around who created this Bellini offshoot. Many people think it was first created at Harry's Bar (see page 49), but according to Maurizio Stocchetto (current Bar Basso owner), it was invented in Milan. The drink itself, named after nineteenth-century Italian composer Gioachino Rossini, is simple to make, easy to drink, and incredibly delicious. The sweet strawberries mixed with prosecco is refreshing and smooth and works wonders as an aperitif but it's also the perfect brunch cocktail if you want to change things up from bottomless mimosas.

✳

**GLASSWARE:** Champagne flute
**GARNISH:** Fresh strawberry

- 4 fresh strawberries
- 1 teaspoon sugar
- ½ oz. fresh lemon juice
- 4 oz. prosecco

1. In a cocktail shaker, muddle the strawberries with the sugar and lemon juice until they are well mashed.

2. Add some crushed ice to the shaker and shake vigorously.

3. Strain the mixture into a Champagne flute.

4. Add the prosecco and gently stir with a barspoon.

5. Garnish with a fresh strawberry.

# GARIBALDI

DANTE NYC
79-81 MACDOUGAL ST, NEW YORK, NY 10012

Named after Giuseppe Garibaldi, the Italian general who is widely credited for helping unify Italy, the Garibaldi pays tribute to the famous general, with its red color that matches the color of the red shirts worn by Garibaldi's supporters. There isn't a definitive history of the drink's creator, but its resurgence in popularity can be attributed to bartender Naren Young at Dante in New York (see page 100), who makes a beautiful version. The drink itself couldn't be easier to create, as it combines just two ingredients—fresh-squeezed orange juice and Campari— for a bittersweet and citrusy combo that goes great with brunch.

---

✳

**GLASSWARE:** Highball (Mamo Hi-Ball)

**GARNISH:** Orange wedge

---

• **4 oz. fresh-squeezed orange juice**   • **1 ½ oz. Campari**

**1.** Add the orange juice to a mixing glass. Completely submerge a frother and froth for 30 seconds, or until a layer of foam has formed.

**2.** Remove the foam with a spoon into a separate glass.

**3.** Fill a highball glass with ice.

**4.** Add the Campari.

**5.** Pour the remaining orange juice into the glass and gently stir.

**6.** Spoon the orange juice foam on top. Garnish with an orange wedge.

# HUGO

BROTHER WOLF
108 W JACKSON AVE #1, KNOXVILLE, TN 37902

There aren't a lot of cocktails that are considered Italian classics, but the Hugo, created in 2005 by bartender Roland Gruber at the Sanzeno bar in South Tyrol, Italy, is one of them. Elderflower is fairly common to the region and Fiorente makes a not-too-sweet liqueur out of the flower that works really well with prosecco and seltzer. You might ask, "Do I really need two types of bubbles for this cocktail?" Well, part of the point of the seltzer is to dilute the sweetness of the liqueur, but it also brings an extra level of fizziness that prosecco alone can't provide. Trust me, it works.

✳

**GLASSWARE: Wine glass**

**GARNISH: Sprig of mint**

- **1 oz. Fiorente Elderflower Liqueur**
- **3 oz. prosecco**
- **2 oz. seltzer**

1. Fill a wine glass with ice, add all the ingredients, and lightly stir.

2. Garnish with a large sprig of mint, gently compressing the leaves to release the oil.

# IL CARDINALE

The Cardinale was invented in 1950 by Giovanni Raimondo at the Excelsior Hotel in Rome. The story goes that it was made for a visiting Cardinal from Germany. But whatever the origin (there are competing claims of versions from 1926 and 1947, of course), the Cardinale is really just a Negroni that uses dry vermouth instead of sweet and is a bit lighter in color. Accordingly, the taste is less sweet than a Negroni, so if your taste buds lend themselves to less sugary vibes, you might want to give Il Cardinale a try.

✳

**GLASSWARE: Rocks glass**

**GARNISH: Lemon zest**

- 1 oz. gin
- ½ oz. Campari
- ¾ oz. Cinzano Extra Dry Vermouth

1. Fill a rocks glass with ice.

2. Pour all the ingredients directly into the rocks glass and stir.

3. Garnish with lemon zest.

# CAFFÈ GILLI

Known as the oldest café in Florence, Caffè Gilli was first opened in 1733 as a pastry shop called a Bozzolari near the famous Duomo. As it expanded and moved locations around Florence, the café became a popular meeting spot for the city's intelligentsia. In 1917, the shop moved into its current location in Piazza della Repubblica and served everything from pastries and coffee to confectionaries. During World War II, the café was also considered a symbol of the resistance movement against the occupying German forces. There are some sources that maintain that Gilli was used as a refuge for Jews and as a central meeting point for Italian resistance fighters.

Today, Gilli is widely known for its confectionaries, chocolates, biscuits, holiday panettone, and more. But that's not what we're here to talk about. The café also has an incredible cocktail bar.

The bar is celebrated for having intricate cocktails that lean into seasonal products, new-age infusions, homemade syrups, and more. The lead bartender is Luca Picchi, awarded as the Bar Manager of the Year at the Bar Awards in 2019 and is one of the world's leading experts on Negronis—he's even written a book, *Negroni Cocktail: An Italian Legend*. You'll find some of the creations here like his NEG-MEX (see page 70), a stellar version of a Mezcal Negroni.

Together with the current bar manager Luca Manni, the team continues to innovate and create new concoctions in this classic spot.

Caffè Gilli lead bartender Luca Picchi

# NEGRONI FLEUR DE LYS

CAFFÈ GILLI
VIA ROMA, IR, 50123 FIRENZE FI, ITALY

World-renowned bartender Luca Picchi is known for his variety of Negronis, and this particular version is one of a kind. Picchi replaces Campari with Amaro Santoni for extra bitterness but then brings in the flavors of apple juice and the licorice-forward star anise to balance against the herbal essence of the gin and dry vermouth. It's a multilayered concoction that Picchi describes as a "fruity, delicate, springtime creation. A light Negroni that is very delicate with a balsamic touch."

**GLASSWARE:** Old-fashioned glass
**GARNISH:** Lemon twist, slice of green apple, 1 or 2 edible flowers

- ⅔ oz. Panarea Island Gin
- ½ oz. Amaro Santoni
- ⅔ oz. Baldoria Bianco Vermouth
- ⅓ oz. Star Anise Syrup (see recipe)
- ⅔ oz. clear apple juice

1. Fill an old-fashioned glass with ice.
2. Add all the ingredients and stir.
3. Garnish with a lemon twist, slice of green apple, and edible flowers.

# STAR ANISE SYRUP

Crush 13 ½ oz. star anise with a mortar and pestle. In a large pot, combine the crushed star anise with 2 liters water and bring the mixture to a boil. Reduce the heat and simmer for 30 minutes. Allow the mixture to cool, then strain it through a fine-mesh strainer. Combine with 600 grams granulated white sugar and stir until the sugar is dissolved.

# NEG-MEX

CAFFÈ GILLI
VIA ROMA, 1R, 50123 FIRENZE FI, ITALY

Though it's known as the oldest bar in Florence (see page 66), that doesn't mean Caffè Gilli isn't coming up with new cocktails. This version of a Negroni uses mezcal in place of gin for a smokier profile, and it also gets more bitter with some coffee liqueur—it's a really nice and unexpected touch.

---

✳

**GLASSWARE:** Old-Fashioned glass
**GARNISH:** Roasted marshmallow, lemon twist, blueberry

---

- ⅔ oz. Alpha Centauri Espadin Mezcal
- ⅔ oz. Campari
- ⅔ oz. Antica Torino Vermouth
- ⅓ oz. Varnelli Caffè Moka Liqueur
- 3 dashes Angostura bitters

1. Fill an old-fashioned glass with ice.

2. Add all the ingredients and stir.

3. Garnish with a roasted marshmallow, a lemon twist, and a blueberry.

# IL BOMBARDINO (THE BOMB)

EATALY

200 5TH AVE, NEW YORK, NY 10010

This classic recipe is courtesy of Eataly and should become your go-to après-ski beverage. The drink was invented in the northern Lombardy region, home to the Italian Alps. According to Eataly, "The legend of the Bombardino is that it was created by a young man from the port city of Genova, who decided to leave the sea for a life in the Italian Alps. After spending years as an officer in the Alpini (the oldest active mountain infantry in the world), he opened a ski lodge. One day, four skiers staggered in from a blizzard, seeking something warm and rich to counteract the cold. The Genovese quickly stirred together milk, whiskey, and zabaglione (an egg-based custard) and brought the ingredients almost to a boiling point. One of the skiers tried the drink and cried, 'Accidenti! È una bomba!' ('Damn! It's a bomb!'). Ever since, skiers traveled far and wide to taste the Genovese's signature drink: Il Bombardino. Over time, the recipe was perfected with a creamy egg liqueur stirred into choice brandy and all topped with whipped cream and cinnamon."

\* 

**GLASSWARE:** Glass coffee mug

**GARNISH:** Whipped cream, cinnamon

- 3 oz. egg liqueur
- 1 ½ oz. Vecchia Romagna Brandy

1. Warm the egg liqueur in a small saucepan.

2. Pour the brandy into a glass coffee mug.

3. When the egg liqueur is hot but not boiling, slowly add it to the brandy and stir well.

4. Top with whipped cream and cinnamon.

# BOULEVARDIER

The Boulevardier, invented around 1927 by writer Erskine Gwynne, has become part of the classic Italian cocktail canon. The drink is easy to remember, as it has equal parts vermouth, bourbon, and aperitivo (the Gwynne version is made with Campari). Similar to the Negroni (replacing gin with bourbon) the Select iteration of the cocktail adds a little more complexity to the drink, as its aperitivo is more bitter and has hints of vanilla.

---

✳

**GLASSWARE:** Rocks glass

**GARNISH:** Orange peel

---

- 1 oz. Select Aperitivo
- 1 oz. sweet vermouth
- 1 oz. bourbon

1. Place a large ice cube in a rocks glass.

2. Combine all the ingredients in a mixing glass. Add ice and stir for 30 seconds.

3. Strain the cocktail into the rocks glass over the ice.

4. Garnish with an orange peel.

# THE GODFATHER

DISARONNO
SARONNO, ITALY

Disaronno Originale (Amaretto Disaronno) is known around the world for its sweet almond-y flavor (though no almonds are used in the making of the liqueur—see page 208). The soft-smokiness and smoothness of the Irish whiskey gives this classic cocktail its notoriously-named taste. The history of this drink is a bit mysterious, but its popularity soared when the movie *The Godfather* was released in 1972. Disaronno even claims the cocktail was one of Marlon Brando's favorites. It's a bit of a chicken-and-egg conundrum, but the cocktail should be considered a classic regardless of its murky beginnings.

**GLASSWARE: Rocks glass**

**GARNISH: Orange twist**

- 1 ½ oz. Busker Blended Irish Whiskey
- ¾ oz. Disaronno Originale

**1.** Combine all the ingredients in a mixing glass with ice.

**2.** Strain the cocktail into a rocks glass over ice.

**3.** Garnish with an orange twist.

# FUTURIST MIXOLOGY

Maybe you've heard of Futurism, founded by Filippo Tommaso Marinetti in the early twentieth century in Italy as a movement to break away from the past and embrace modernity and technology. Maybe you're familiar with some of the art and architecture coming out of this cultural moment by Umberto Boccioni and Giacomo Balla. And maybe you know them as being friends with the Italian Fascists at the time. But what you might not realize is that Marinetti and his Futurist followers dabbled in food and drink as well.

Marinetti published the Futurist Manifesto in 1909, which gradually had an impact on all walks of Italian cultural life. Chronicled in the book *Futurist Mixology: Polibibite, the Autarkic Italian Answer to the Cocktails of the 1930s*, by Fulvio Piccinino are nearly two dozen cocktails created by the writers and artists of Futurism that fell into a few separate buckets and were all meant to shock and awe their drinking audiences.

*Polibibite* is the name the Futurists gave to this collection of drinks. The cocktails were broken into the following categories: *Aperitifs* for appetite stimulation, *War in Bed* to stimulate procreation (literally), *Peace in Bed* to give you calm, *Early to Bed* for cold winter nights, *Fog Lifters* for freeing the mind of useless morals, and *Inventina* for new and original ideas.

Because the cocktails were invented by artists, and not by traditional bartenders, they tend to look better than they taste. But I've included three of the recipes in the book, the Decisone (see page 81), which is a *Fog Lifter*, Il Rigeneratore (see page 82), which is a *War in Bed* cocktail, and the Coppa Di Brividi (see page 85), an *Aperitif*.

These cocktails are truly a blast from the past with an eye on the future, and make for really great conversation starters. Have fun making these unique concoctions and check out Piccinino's book to get all nineteen recipes. You can also find more information on these cocktails at the Cocchi (see page 166) website, who is also the publisher of *Futurist Mixology*.

reated by Futurism movement founder Filippo Tommaso Marinetti, the Decisone is not spelled wrong; in fact, it's meant to signify a big decision. This drink is supposed to be served warm, though you can certainly make it on ice in a low tumbler. When you warm this cocktail, the ingredients will meld together, and the result will be citrusy, sweet, and slightly earthy. It's one of the few polibibite cocktails that would hold up well today and falls under the *Fog Lifter* category of Futurist drinks that were designed to loosen your morals.

**GLASSWARE:** Rialto coupe (SIR/MADAM)
**GARNISH:** Mandarin peel

- ¾ oz. Cocchi Barolo Chinato
- ¾ oz. Barolo DOCG
- ¾ oz. mandarin juice
- ¾ oz. aged rhum

1. Combine all the ingredients in a low pot and heat on a stovetop over medium-low heat.

2. Strain the cocktail into a Rialto coupe.

3. Garnish with a mandarin peel.

# IL RIGENERATORE (THE REGENERATOR)

Created by one of Futurism's biggest advocates, Cinzio Barosi, the Il Rigeneratore was supposed to be a cooking recipe, but the addition of Asti Spumante categorized it as a drink. According to Piccinino, "Futurist mixes had constant, fairly explicit, sexual references, with the clear aim of exciting diners and encouraging fecundation, for the creation of the 'future Italian people.'" The name Rigeneratore is part of the *War in Bed* category of Futurist drinks, and the ingredients in this cocktail were meant to give men a second wind in the sack. Whether that works or not, it's a really fun and very phallic cocktail to experiment with.

---

✳

**GLASSWARE:** Old-fashioned glass (Atelier Crestani)

**GARNISH:** Banana

---

- 1 egg yolk
- 3 teaspoons sugar
- 3 roasted walnuts
- 3 ⅓ oz. Moscato d'Asti DOCG

1. In a bowl, beat the egg with the sugar until the mixture becomes thick and whitish, 4 to 5 minutes.

2. Add the egg mixture and roasted walnuts to a blender and blend until only small walnut pieces remain.

3. Slowly pour the mixture into a mixing glass with ice and add the moscato. Stir.

4. Strain the cocktail into an old-fashioned glass.

5. Garnish by placing a whole banana in the middle of the glass.

# COPPA DI BRIVIDI (GLASS OF SHIVERS)

This recipe was created by Futurist painter, poet, and sculptor Fortunato Depero, who thought artists should also be creative geniuses in the culinary and mixology worlds. There's not a lot of genius to this drink, however—it's a slight copy of the sugar-rimmed Brandy Crusta, mixed with a Harvard or a Metropolitan, which combines vermouth and brandy, as well. Either way, this simple-to-make cocktail is sweet and fruity with just a hint of bitterness and is a nice aperitif to sip and reminisce about Italy in the 1930s, before fascism ruined everything.

---
✳
---

**GLASSWARE:** Nick & Nora glass (Chef&Sommelier)
**GARNISH:** 4 grapes, 2 pear wedges, 1 orange wheel (all refrigerated)

- Sugar, for the glass rim
- ¾ oz. Italian brandy
- 1 ¼ oz. Cocchi Storico Vermouth di Torino

1. Rim a Nick & Nora glass with sugar.

2. Add the grapes and pear pieces to the glass.

3. Add the brandy and vermouth to a mixing glass with ice and stir.

4. Strain the mixture into the glass.

5. Float an orange wheel on the surface of the liquid.

# APERITIVO:

# THE ART OF PRE-DINNER
# (AND MORE) DRINKING IN ITALY

APEROL-SPRITZ

BLACK MANHATTAN

FLOP

AY QUE RICO

SEVILLE SPRITZ

SICILIAN SBAGLIATO

TROPICAL BIRD SPRITZ

STAZIONE TONIC

Hey Paul, let's go have an aperitivo for our aperitivo during aperitivo, said cocktail expert and Italian cocktail historian Livio Lauro.

What does *that* mean?

Aperitivo is three things all at once and Lauro breaks it down like this: "The problem with the term 'aperitivo' is, number one, it can simply mean anything that you drink before a meal. Number two, the aperitivo is also a time of day. It's a ritual of getting together before eating, which in Italy is twice a day. We're not a 9 to 5 country; we are an 8 to 1, 4 to 7country. So, when you're in a big city and you get off work at 1 p.m., you're going to just go down the street to the aperitivo hour to drink and socialize. Number three, the beverages that are actually labeled with the term 'aperitivo.' We're talking about Aperol, Select, Contratto. Is Campari an aperitivo? No, because Campari is labeled as a bitter, but you can drink a bitter such as Campari as an aperitivo."

Now that that's clear (is it?), let's talk a bit about history. The reason the term "aperitivo" exists is rooted in the Latin word *aperitivus*, which means "something that opens," and for this purpose, opening the stomach and promoting an appetite. Italian historian Giammario Villa traces this ritual to Roman and pre-Roman times. "You have to look at the production of scented wines with a mild bitter taste. In fact, it's a bitter taste that stimulates the appetite, not a sweet taste. Also in ancient Roman times there was *mulsum*, a mix of wine (high in alcohol) and aromatized honey paired with savory appetizers and served during the *gustatio*, the opening moment of important banquets."

Villa explains that the tradition of socializing with drinks before a meal can't be pinpointed exactly, but during the eighteenth century, Antonio Benedetto Carpano created a vermouth for the purpose of an aperitif. Subsequently, it was adopted as a royal aperitif by King Vittorio Emanuele II, which gave this up-and-coming trend of aperitivo the boost toward what we see today.

The eighteenth and nineteenth centuries saw the rise of every prominent Italian brand we know of today—Campari, Martini & Rossi, Liquore Strega, Lucano, Fernet-Branca, and many others—which gave rise to café culture in Milan and the ritual of aperitivo as a time to stimulate your appetite before a meal.

Cut to today, where you can have an aperitivo, for your aperitivo, during aperitivo, at bars all over Italy and around the world—often with a buffet of food to go alongside. For the purposes of this book, I refer to the drink you have during this time as an "aperitif," to make things less confusing (does it?), and the following cocktail recipes are the ideal versions of these pre-meal drinks to open up your stomach and prepare for a great feast and an even greater night ahead.

# APEROL

## PADUA, ITALY

Aperol is one of the most recognizable brands in the world and is widely credited with launching the groundbreaking idea of an aperitif with a lower ABV, consisting of only eleven percent alcohol. Created in 1919 by brothers Silvio and Luigi Barbieri, the tantalizing orange concoction quickly grew into a global phenomenon.

Aperol is made with a secret recipe of herbs and roots and has a unique bittersweet taste that's infused with citrus peels and essential oils.

As you're probably familiar, the signature drink in the Aperol portfolio is the Aperol Spritz (see page 92). The vivacious cocktail with its easy-to-remember blend of 3 parts prosecco, 2 parts Aperol, and 1 part seltzer has become the go-to summer drink for any and all pre-dinner social hours.

Aperol's official drinking home is Terrazza Aperol, the company's flagship bar in Venice that is the ideal spot to engage in the traditional ritual of aperitivo. The bar opened in 2021 and has a large patio space that looks out on the Campo Santo Stefano and is ideal for small bites and large Spritzes. The bar also offers a masterclass on how to make the perfect Aperol Spritz while you sail along the Grand Canal in an historical boat with a bartender on board.

Today, Aperol is part of the Campari Group's brand portfolio, which has only supercharged its popularity and ubiquitousness in the aperitivo space.

# APEROL SPRITZ

TERRAZZA APEROL
CAMPO SANTO STEFANO, 2776, 30124 VENEZIA VE,
ITALY

The official drink of summer, the Aperol Spritz has soared in popularity around the world over the past decade and for good reason—it's perfect. The history of this iconic drink is a little vague—though it was originally a colorless cocktail and was likely influenced by the Venetian Spritz, which was created in the 1920s and inspired by soldiers in the Austrian empire who would water down Venetian wines with seltzer to cut the high alcohol content. It wasn't until the 1950s, however, that the Aperol Spritz that we know today came about with its signature 3-2-1 ratio of prosecco-Aperol-seltzer. Today, it symbolizes the Italian lifestyle of drinking an aperitif before dinner, socializing with friends, and getting a night started on a very refreshing foot.

**GLASSWARE:** Wine glass

**GARNISH:** Orange slice

- 3 oz. Cinzano Prosecco
- 2 oz. Aperol
- 1 oz. seltzer

1. Fill a wine glass with ice.

2. Add to the glass in the following order: prosecco, Aperol, then seltzer.

3. Garnish with an orange slice.

# BLACK MANHATTAN

AVERNA
CALTANISSETTA, SICILY

The classic Manhattan is made with red vermouth, bourbon, and bitters. The Black Manhattan changes things up a tad by replacing the vermouth with Amaro Averna but keeping the ratios of 2-1 bourbon-amaro the same as the traditional recipe. What you get here is a less-sweet version of this cocktail but with some added spice and bitterness. It's a very classy drink that goes well before or after dinner.

**GLASSWARE:** Coupe glass, chilled
**GARNISH:** Brandied cherry

- 1 oz. Amaro Averna
- 2 dashes Angostura bitters
- 2 oz. Russell's Reserve 6-Year Rye

1. Add all the ingredients to a mixer with ice and stir.

2. Strain the cocktail into the coupe.

3. Garnish with a brandied cherry.

# FRENI E FRIZIONI

## VIA DEL POLITEAMA, 4, 00153 ROMA RM, ITALY

If there's any bar that symbolizes the aperitivo scene in Rome, it's Freni e Frizioni. They call themselves a street cocktail bar, and that's exactly what you'll find as you cross the Ponte Sisto to the west side of the Tiber River. Tucked into a corner just across the street from the river, you'll happen upon Freni's outdoor yellow and red tables and a young crowd of drinkers all sharing in the ritual of the pre-dinner drink.

Effortlessly cool, the cocktails here aren't your typical spritzes (though you can get those, too), but stunningly creative concoctions that whet your appetite in surprisingly fun ways. But Freni is probably most well-known in Rome for introducing a massive buffet to go along with the drinks. I was able to talk to Riccardo Rossi at Freni to get a little more insight into this Roman staple of pre-dinner culture.

### Tell me about your aperitivo—what makes it fun/unique/different?

Freni e Frizioni was one of the first bars that focused on aperitivo. The aperitivo was a tradition coming from the North of Italy, especially in Turin and Milan. Our buffet formula (food included in the price of the drink) was a success from day one and that made our bar a high volume venue. The formula hasn't really changed since then and even now you can enjoy our aperitivo every day from 6:30 p.m. to 9:30 p.m.

### Tell me about aperitivo culture in Rome.

The aperitivo culture in Rome started a bit later than the northern region of Italy. Now almost every bar has its own formula. There are places that offer you little bites with your drinks, others they make you pay for them and then there are bars like us with the buffet. In general, I'd say that the aperitivo time in Italy is a kind of ritual. It can represent the end of a day or the start of a night.

Regarding the drinks, the Spritz is maybe the best-selling cocktail during that time but in the last few years we saw the sale of Negroni and Americano growing exponentially.

# FLOP

FRENI E FRIZIONI
VIA DEL POLITEAMA, 4, 00153 ROMA RM, ITALY

Known in Rome as one of the best aperitivo spots, Freni e Frizioni has a wide array of original cocktail creations. The Flop is one of their most interesting drinks that combines sour, bitter, and sweet flavors in wonderful ways. The tequila they use is a fun choice because it's particularly smoky, while the spicy salt rim will bring a little heat and a savory kick after each sip. If this doesn't get you in the mood for dinner, I don't know what else to tell you.

---

* ✳ *

**GLASSWARE:** Coupette
**GARNISH:** Spicy salt, for the rim

---

- 1 oz. Tequila Curado Espadín
- ½ oz. amaretto liqueur
- 1 oz. white bitter
- 4/5 oz. lemon juice
- ½ oz. bitter orange and rhubarb syrup

1. Rim a coupette with spicy salt.

2. Add all the ingredients to a cocktail shaker with ice and shake vigorously for 15 seconds.

3. Double-strain the cocktail into the coupette.

# AY QUE RICO

FRENI E FRIZIONI
VIA DEL POLITEAMA, 4, 00153 ROMA RM, ITALY

The name of this cocktail means "Oh So Rich" in Spanish and that's pretty fitting. There's a good amount of spice in this drink, but the richness can be found in the blending of the smoky tequila, the sweet and spicy flavors of the falernum, and the tart cordial. It's a very well-rounded, slightly citrusy cocktail that should make you think of beachy locales, preferably on the Italian Riviera or an island off the coast of Spain.

---

※

**GLASSWARE: Lowball glass**

**GARNISH: Caper fruit**

---

- 1 ½ oz. Curado Tequila Cupreata
- ½ oz. falernum
- ⅓ oz. Ancho Reyes redistilled with sage
- ⅔ oz. passion fruit and capers cordial
- ⅔ oz. lime juice

1. Place a large single cube of ice in a lowball glass.
2. Add all the ingredients to a cocktail shaker with ice and shake.
3. Strain the cocktail into the lowball glass.
4. Garnish with a caper fruit.

# DANTE NYC

## 79-81 MACDOUGAL ST, NEW YORK, NY 10012

Arguably the most important bar in America when it comes to Italian cocktails, many credit Dante with helping to popularize the Negroni in the U.S. That and many other reasons are why it was named the World's Best Bar in 2019 (and continues to remain on the Top 50 list to this day).

This Greenwich Village mainstay first opened as Caffe Dante in 1915 in the heart of an Italian neighborhood. Over the years, the bar has seen no shortage of celebrity regulars, like Al Pacino, Jerry Seinfeld, and Alex Baldwin, but also old-school luminaries like Ernest Hemingway, Bob Dylan, Robert Mapplethorpe, and Patti Smith.

Dante is registered as a New York Landmark and can claim one of the best bar programs in America. Italophiles flock here for their perfect Negroni and Garibaldi, but also for their signature cocktails which feature more than half a dozen Spritzes and Negroni off-shoots, as well as a great selection of digestifs to work off their pastas and flatbreads.

Oozing with history of the Italian American experience but thriving as a bar with an eye on the future, this Italian cocktail spot bridges the Atlantic with authenticity and originality and continues to be a trendsetter in the world of Italian drinks.

# SEVILLE SPRITZ

DANTE NYC
79-81 MACDOUGAL ST, NEW YORK, NY 10012

Known for its elaborate Italian-based cocktails, Dante in New York City is consistently ranked in the top 50 best bars in the world. Their Seville Spritz is just one of many reasons they maintain that top spot. Combining the orange flavors of Tanqueray's gin, curaçao, orange wine, orange, bitters, and orange blossom—plus a blood orange and orange twist garnish—it simply refreshes like a great Spritz should.

**GLASSWARE:** Highball
**GARNISH:** Blood orange wheel, orange twist

- 1 oz. Tanqueray Sevilla Gin
- 1 oz. orange wine
- ½ oz. vanilla syrup
- 2 dashes orange bitters
- ½ oz. Pierre Ferrand Dry Curaçao
- 1 drop orange blossom
- 3 oz. prosecco

1. Fill a highball glass with ice.

2. In a cocktail shaker with ice, combine all the ingredients except the prosecco and shake vigorously.

3. Strain the drink into the highball glass.

4. Top with prosecco and gently stir.

5. Garnish with a blood orange wheel and an orange twist.

# SICILIAN SBAGLIATO

DANTE NYC
79-81 MACDOUGAL ST, NEW YORK, NY 10012

**D**on't confuse this cocktail with a Negroni Sbagliato; the ingredients are vastly different and range from Luxardo's bitter orange Bianco and Dolin Blanc dry vermouth to Dante's homegrown limoncello and the bubbly vivaciousness of prosecco and San Pellegrino. It'll refresh while giving you loads of citrus to ponder. Get transported to New York with this fun aperitif.

**GLASSWARE:** Highball glass
**GARNISH:** Lemon flower

- ¾ oz. Luxardo Bitter Bianco
- ¾ oz. Dolin Blanc Vermouth
- ½ oz. Dante Limoncello
- 2 dashes lemon bitters
- 2 ½ oz. prosecco
- ½ oz. San Pellegrino

1. Fill a highball with one rectangular ice chunk.
2. Fill a shaker with ice and add the Luxardo, Dolin Blanc, limoncello, and lemon bitters and shake vigorously for 10 to 15 seconds.
3. Strain the mixture into the highball glass.
4. Top the drink with prosecco and San Pellegrino and gently stir.
5. Garnish with a lemon flower.

@dantenewyorkcity

# TROPICAL BIRD SPRITZ

MARTINI & ROSSI
PIAZZA LUIGI ROSSI, 2 10023 PESSIONE DI CHIERI
TORINO TO, ITALY

This Spritz is a really fun way to start off an evening. The vermouth is nice and bitter, the elderflower liqueur is sweet, the pineapple is tart and fruity, and the prosecco and soda water provide the bubbles. What more can you ask for as you snack on apps before indulging in an Italian feast?

❋

**GLASSWARE:** Collins glass

**GARNISH:** Lime wheel

- 1 ½ oz. Martini & Rossi Riserva Speciale Bitter Vermouth
- 1 oz. Martini & Rossi Prosecco
- 1 oz. soda water
- ½ oz. St-Germain Elderflower Liqueur
- ½ oz. pineapple shrub

1. Add all the ingredients to a collins glass with ice and stir.

2. Garnish with a lime wheel.

# STAZIONE TONIC

LIQUORE STREGA
PIAZZA VITTORIA COLONNA, 8, 82100 BENEVENTO BN,
ITALY

Fans of Gin & Tonics will love this variation of the classic cocktail. Adding Liquore Strega, bartender Alex Frezza (of L'Antiquario bar in Naples) gives the old standby a sweeter flavor with a minty finish.

---

✳

**GLASSWARE:** Tumbler glass, chilled

**GARNISH:** Lime wedge

---

- 1 oz. Liquore Strega
- 1 oz. gin
- 4 oz. tonic water

1. Fill a tumbler with ice cubes.

2. Add the Liquore Strega and gin, and then slowly add the tonic water to save its effervescence.

3. Garnish with a lime wedge.

## TIP FROM ALEX FREZZA

Today the market offers many kinds of tonic waters—try to have fun by changing the type of tonic in this drink. Start with a neutral tonic and then try a spicier one with Mediterranean herbs. In this case, change the garnish as well, using a lemon rind from Sorrento and a small branch of rosemary.

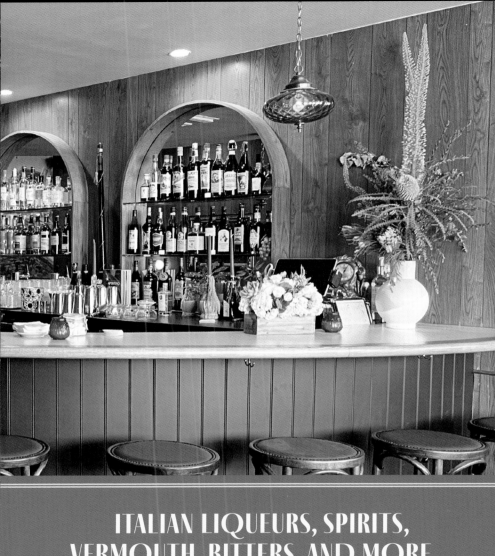

# ITALIAN LIQUEURS, SPIRITS, VERMOUTH, BITTERS, AND MORE

| | |
|---|---|
| COMPADRE | ORPHIC FLOWERS |
| CAMPARI SELTZ | THE RAIN NYMPH |
| AMERICANO BOLOGNESE | SOUR CHERRY MARTINEZ |
| VERMUTTINO | IMPROVED LAST WORD |
| PAPER PLANE | SCHÜMLI PFLÜMLI |
| MERLOT MOJITO | HEARTS AND DAGGERS |
| COFFEE NEGRONI | IL PIEMONTESE |
| EA SENSATION | CINZANO LA NUOVA TORINO |
| DICIOTTO 60 | MEZCALICUS |
| FIVE O'CLOCK | ITALICUS CUP |
| BRANCAMILANO | DISARONNO SOUR |
| FERNET CUP N.1 | DISARONNO FIZZ |
| SARPARITA | CYNAR JULEP |
| VE.N.TO | CYNAR MANHATTAN |
| MONTE & MEZCAL | BALDORIA DRY & TONIC |
| MONTE MANHATTAN | DRY UMAMI SHERRY COBBLER |
| LIMONATA | SMOKE & BITTERS |
| MIDNIGHT TO MIDNIGHT | BROKEN BICYCLETTE |
| ROSA ROSITA | ITALIAN HANDSHAKE |
| EXTRA SONIC | HAZELNUT OLD FASHIONED |
| AROMA | |
| SLIPPERY NIPPLE | |
| FORMIDABILE NEGRONI | |

If you pay close attention to the shelves behind the bartenders at any bar in the world, you'll notice something that they all have in common: Italian products. You can't go to a bar, basically anywhere on the planet, that doesn't have a bottle of Campari, or Fernet-Branca, Martini & Rossi vermouth, or any number of Italian liqueurs.

Many drinkers probably take for granted how vast the Italian liqueur canon truly is. But when you think about it, and I mean really think about it, cocktailing would be really difficult without Italy's contributions. I'm talking about vermouth, amaretto, bitters, aperitivos, prosecco, limoncello, sambuca, grappa, and the hundreds if not thousands of amari. Galliano? Italian. Frangelico? Italian. Liquore Strega? Italian. The list goes on and on and on.

In this chapter, I highlight many of the oldest, best, and most interesting Italian producers that are the engine behind almost every great drink you've ever had.

# CAMPARI

There is no more important brand to the world of Italian cocktails than Campari. Founded by Gaspare Campari in 1860, the original concoction came after years of experimentation with the infusions of bitter herbs, aromatic plants, different fruits, and alcohol. The iconic red color was also the result of a dye that was obtained from the cochineal insect (they use different dyes today).

In 1904, Campari erected its first manufacturing plant in Milan, kicking off a mass production that would lead to worldwide domination in multiple spirits categories. Today the Campari Group is one of the biggest spirits companies in the world, and owns and produces Aperol (see page 91), Skyy Vodka, Grand Marnier, Wild Turkey, Cynar (see page 213), Averna (see page 161), Frangelico (see page 231), Cinzano (see page 198), and dozens of other brands.

When it comes to cocktails, Campari is a mainstay in a wide range of classics. Everything from the Negroni (see page 29) and Americano (see page 30) to the Boulevardier (see page 75) and Garibaldi (see page 61) are all traditionally made with Campari, giving the drinks their subtle bitterness.

# COMPADRE

CAMPARINO IN GALLERIA
P.ZA DEL DUOMO, 21, 20121 MILANO MI, ITALY

The Compadre is a featured drink inside the contemporary Sala Spiritello, the modern of the two bars at Camparino in Galleria (see page 42). The smoky Compadre is the perfect illustration of the company's past meeting the future of mixology by combining the bittersweetness of Campari with the earthiness and pepperiness of the mezcal. It's almost like a ping pong ball in your mouth as the flavors dance from bitter to sweet to roasted to floral. Enjoy.

**GLASSWARE:** Tumbler glass (shallow Riedel), chilled

**GARNISH:** Kaffir lime leaf

- 1 ¼ oz. Campari
- ⅔ oz. Montelobos Mezcal Espadìn
- ½ oz. Quaglia Chinotto Liqueur
- ½ oz. 1757 Vermouth di Torino Rosso
- 2 dashes Angostura bitters
- 2 sprays of bergamot essence

1. Place a giant ice cube inside a tumbler.
2. Fill a mixing glass with the Campari, mezcal, Quaglia Chinotto Liqueur, red vermouth, and bitters.
3. Add 7 to 8 ice cubes and stir for about 10 to 15 seconds.
4. Strain and pour the cocktail into the tumbler.
5. Garnish with a kaffir lime leaf and spray with essence of bergamot.

# CAMPARI SELTZ

CAMPARINO IN GALLERIA
P.ZA DEL DUOMO, 21, 20121 MILANO MI, ITALY

The simplest of drinks, the chilled Campari Seltz is a bittersweet aperitif with some bubbles. The Campari Seltz is Bar di Passo's (see page 42) signature drink because it symbolizes the history of Campari and the classic, simple way of making a really great cocktail.

* * *

**GLASSWARE:** Tulip glass, chilled

- 3 oz. Campari, chilled
- Seltzer, to top

**1.** Pour the chilled Campari into the chilled tulip glass.

**2.** Slowly pour the seltzer into the glass to top off the drink.

# MARTINI & ROSSI

You really can't talk about Italian cocktails without mentioning one of its most important legacy brands, Martini & Rossi. The vintage vermouth company was founded in Turin, Italy in 1863 by three men, Alessandro Martini, Luigi Rossi, and Teofilo Sola. The company was originally called Martini, Sola, & Cia, but once the Sola family sold their interests in 1879, the name Martini & Rossi was established.

There's so much history to this company that there are entire books written about them. But for the purposes of this book, I was able to talk to Anna Scudellari, Heritage Curator at Martini & Rossi, to get insight into how they came to be. Scudellari manages the company's archive collection, museum collection, and book collections.

Follow along and then dive into the really fun M&R recipes on the next few pages.

### Can you tell me about the origin of the company?

We have three founders, Alessandro Martini, Teofilo Sola, and Luigi Rossi and they were a dream team. They worked very well together because they had different skills. Martini was a salesman; he was also a skilled public relations person, and he became a sort of ambassador for the brand. He pushed for an international expansion of the brand and the products almost immediately. He died in 1905 and after his death, the Rossi family became the only owner of the company. The second founder was Teofilo Sola. He was born in a town near Turin and was focused on the administrative management of the company, but he died early when he was just 48 years old. After his death, his three children didn't follow in their father's footsteps, so the company at this stage was renamed Martini & Rossi.

The third partner, Luigi Rossi, is probably the key person in this story. He was born in 1828 in a small town near Turin. He moved to Turin to learn the secrets of herbs and liqueurs and create his job in this sector. After a short apprenticeship, he started his own business and opened a shop of herbs, vermouths, and liqueurs in Turin. He was very well known by the other two partners of the company as a talented herbalist, and as a person able to create aromatic wines in the Turin tradition. So, he became a partner in 1863 and he became the production director. In 1864, he moved to Pessione, which is a small town thirty kilometers from Turin, where the production site was opened, and is still where the production plant is today, still active after 160 years. The great success the company has had was largely due to Luigi's creativity, and the creation of that iconic vermouth recipe.

### When did the vermouth become known as a pivotal cocktail ingredient?

The story moves from Turin to the United States, because, as far as I know, the United States is the place where cocktails were born as a typical way to drink spirits. The [company's] foundation was in 1863 and four years later, [in 1867,] Martini & Rossi was in the United States with its first 100 cases of vermouth rosso. And soon it became the most-exported vermouth to the United States. This is part of the story of the creation of cocktail trends.

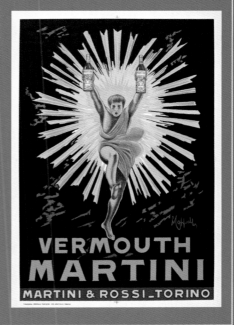

# AMERICANO BOLOGNESE

MARTINI & ROSSI
PIAZZA LUIGI ROSSI, 2 10023 PESSIONE DI CHIERI
TORINO TO, ITALY

Your classic Americano is a simple cocktail made with Campari, sweet vermouth, and soda water. Martini & Rossi changes things up with a special vermouth to replace the Campari, their own Speciale Bitter, along with ginger juice and Angostura bitters. This cocktail will be more complex than the original Americano, definitely spicier, and more bitter, yet equally refreshing.

---

✳

**GLASSWARE:** Highball glass

**GARNISH:** Orange wedge

---

- ¾ oz. Martini & Rossi Riserva Speciale Bitter
- ¾ oz. Martini & Rossi Riserva Speciale Rubino
- ¼ oz. fresh ginger juice
- 3 dashes Angostura bitters
- Soda water, to top

1. Fill a highball with ice.
2. Add all the ingredients, except the bitters and soda water, and stir.
3. Add the bitters and top off with soda water.
4. Garnish with an orange wedge.

# VERMUTTINO

MARTINI & ROSSI
PIAZZA LUIGI ROSSI, 2 10023 PESSIONE DI CHIERI
TORINO TO, ITALY

The combination of vermouth and soda is one of life's simple pleasures. Martini & Rossi makes a perfect not-too-sweet vermouth and when mixed with soda water, it brightens, refreshes, and tickles your nostrils. Great on a late summer afternoon to open up your taste buds before dinner.

✳

**GLASSWARE:** Highball glass

**GARNISH:** Lemon twist

- **2 oz. Martini & Rossi Rosso Sweet Vermouth**
- **3 oz. soda water**

1. Fill a highball with ice.

2. Add the vermouth, top with soda water, and stir.

3. Garnish with lemon twist.

# NONINO

If you know anything about grappa, you know the name Nonino. While they're not the first widely produced grappa distiller, they are the first to make a premium single-varietal grappa. They're also the first grappa distiller to be run by women, as Silvia Nonino took over the reins in the 1940s when her husband, Antonio Nonino, died.

That tradition of women running things carries on to this day as the company is helmed by Cristina, Antonella, Elisabetta, and Francesca Nonino, who are bringing grappa into the future and creating legions of fans for this spirit that was once known as just a peasant liquor.

Nonino was started in 1897 by Orazio Nonino in northern Italy. Nonino used a moveable still to extract grappa from wine stems, skins, and seeds (pomace). That process has obviously been refined many times since. Traditionally, grappa was consumed as a post-dinner digestif, but as the quality continued to get better over time, it became a fascinating ingredient in cocktails. Nonino provided multiple recipes that range from a version of a Mojito (see page 130) to a take on a Spritz (see page 44). The recipes are multilayered and incredibly dynamic.

I was able to speak with Francesca Nonino about the company's past, its innovations, and its future.

### Let's start with the history of Nonino.

We have been a family of distillers since 1897. My family is famous all over the world because my grandmother and grandfather, Giannola and Benito Nonino, revolutionized the way of making grappa. When we're talking about grappa, we're talking about the most ancient and traditional spirit of Italy. To be able to make grappa, you need to be distilling Italian pomace—the leftovers after you press grapes for making wine—and that pomace has to be Italian, and you need to distill it in Italy. Otherwise, it's not grappa. Grappa was born in the thirteenth century when farmers were smart enough to understand that what was considered just a leftover from winemakers could have a second life, because pomace contains sugar, and because it contains sugar, it can be fermented, and because it can be fermented, it could be distilled. But at the time distilling at home was illegal, so they had to wait for a cloudy day so they could cover the alcohol steam and not get caught. Moreover, they were still using direct fire and that means that most of the time they burned the pomace and so what they produced was called not only grappa, but also fire water, which is able to burn away even hunger, just to give you an idea.

So, grappa was not considered something elegant, it was considered a pretty rustic type of spirit, but it was part of everyday life. It was something where you would wake up and it's really cold outside, you drink a little bit of grappa to warm you up. If your tooth ached, you would drink a little bit of grappa. If your baby was crying too much, you put a finger of grappa in their mouth. Grappa was really for solving any type of problem in the farmer's everyday life. But when my grandmother fell in love with my grandfather, she understood that the grappa he was making was completely different. Because my grandfather understood the first rule of distillation, which is that the fresher the raw material you're distilling, the more delicious the final spirit will be. So, he went completely against what was the tradition of stocking the pomace for up to eight months before distilling it. And he decided to build the most unique distillery in the world, with sixty-six artisanal pots to distill the pomace super fresh. He would wait a maximum of an hour and a half before distilling it to really be able to get the soul, the essence of the grape, and put it in the final glass. He built this distillery that instead of distilling for eight months a year, he would only distill for eight weeks per year, exactly during the harvest, but twenty-four hours per day, seven days of the week, to be able to really, really capture the most notable components of the pomace and be able to create spirits that are able to move people to tell the history of our beautiful terroir of our region.

My grandmother and my grandfather decided to do one other thing. It was not only to distill super-fresh pomace, but also to try to distill, for the very first-time, a single varietal grappa. At that time, grappa was made by distilling altogether red and white pomace, mixing them without any type of logic, because pomace was considered just a waste. But they thought that by distilling a single varietal pomace, they could prove to the world that grappa was not this "fire water" but could be the soul, the essence of the grape, in the glass. They were able to distill the very first single varietal grappa in 1973, and they picked a really special one for this trial called *picolit*, which is an indigenous varietal from Friuli that suffers a floral abortion and that means that only a few flowers turn into grapes, but those grapes are full of nutrients, of sugar, and they're almost like a nectar. This vineyard was considered a noble one because it was the vineyard used for making wine for the pope. When they distilled it for the first time, they created what is known today as the legendary Picolit Monovitigno grappa, and they proved to the world what grappa could really be. After that, grappa was transformed into something that today represents Italian excellence all over the world. Distilling single varietals meant there could be many different types of grappa—grappa picolit, moscato, chardonnay, prosecco, merlot—and each of these grappa have a completely different type of personality. And that not only opened up the possibility of using grappa as a digestive, but also as an ingredient in recipes, and also for making cocktails.

**How are you trying to educate people about all this rich history and bring a newer generation into your grappa world?**

What I think is true is that the younger generation doesn't know very much about grappa. But I think that one thing that's really good for us is the fact that consumers nowadays are much more knowledgeable and though they want to drink less, they want to drink better. And that is the type of consumer we want to address. People want to know what they're eating, and what they're drinking, and I think that is the best type of consumer we can have. Nowadays, people drink

less to get drunk. They drink to have an experience, and what I'm here to do is to teach the experience of drinking grappa and the history of drinking it and what it represents, and to mix grappa in a cocktail, because grappa is not just about Italian excellence, but it represents Italian culture. And I think that today, drinking a product that represents our country is part of the experience for the consumer. I think that people are willing more and more to have a genuine, authentic experience with what they're consuming. And I think that there isn't anything more genuine and authentic and Italian than grappa.

# PAPER PLANE

NONINO
VIA AQUILEIA, 104, 33050 PERCOTO UDINE UD, ITALY

You could argue that the modern drinking world was truly introduced to Amaro Nonino when famed New York bartender Sam Ross (also the creator of the Penicillin) invented this cocktail that consists of a maximum of five ingredients, with the same amounts of each in 2007. The Paper Plane is a take on a whiskey sour but adds the bitterness of amaro with the refreshing citrus notes from the Aperol.

**GLASSWARE:** Coupe glass

- ¾ oz. Amaro Nonino Quintessentia
- ¾ oz. Aperol
- ¾ oz. bourbon
- ¾ oz. fresh lemon juice

1. Mix all the ingredients in a cocktail shaker filled with ice.

2. Shake vigorously and strain the cocktail into a coupe.

# MERLOT MOJITO

NONINO

VIA AQUILEIA, 104, 33050 PERCOTO UDINE UD, ITALY

As part of a marketing push, the Nonino family challenged bartenders to "Be brave, mix grappa" and create new cocktail concoctions with the legacy brand. Famed German bartender Jörg Meyer took up the challenge and decided to make a mojito with a twist. The result is the Merlot Mojito, which uses the Grappa Nonino Monovitigno Merlot to give a classic Mojito a subtle sweetness and tartness with an herbal, refreshing, and elegant finish.

**GLASSWARE:** Collins glass

**GARNISH:** Mint sprig

- 2 ½ oz. Grappa Nonino Monovitigno Merlot
- 1 oz. lime juice
- ¾ oz. cane sugar syrup
- 10 mint leaves
- Soda water, to top

1. Fill a collins glass with ice.

2. Fill the glass with all the ingredients and top with soda water.

3. Stir and garnish with a mint sprig.

# TIP

To get more mint flavor into your drink, use a muddler to crush the mint leaves with the lime juice and syrup before adding the other ingredients.

# LUCANO

5, VIA CAV. PASQUALE VENA, PISTICCI,
MT 75015, ITALY

For bartenders in the know, Amaro Lucano is a requirement for any bottle collection. Today, Lucano makes more than just amaro; they have one of the best limoncellos on the market, in addition to great vermouths and grappas. When it comes to cocktails, Lucano Amaro is a mainstay in a bevy of recipes like the EA Sensation (see page 136), a totally unique Coffee Negroni (see page 135), and many more.

I was able to chat with the current co-CEO of Lucano, Leonardo Vena, who is the fourth generation of the family to run things.

### Can you tell me about the history of the company?

My great-grandfather established the company in 1894. Originally, he was a pastry chef from Basilicata, but in the 1880s, moved to Naples where he gained knowledge in botanicals. [After working in Naples,] he opened a small lab in his hometown [to make amaro].

Five years ago, my brother and I each took the position of co-CEO and my first goal was to spread the brand all over the world. We also bought another company called Mancino Vermouth. Our principal product is the amaro and it's been the same recipe since 1894. We have never changed it, of course, and we have to follow strict regulations. There are more than thirty botanicals, but the botanicals don't all go together; we have five different macerations. So, the thirty botanicals are divided into different groups and only my father knows the perfect percent of the recipe. Of course, I know what he does, but the groups of botanicals are named with numbers. So even the old guys don't know the exact amounts of the recipe.

**Do you ever think about how at that time, anyone was able to put that many different ingredients together to come up with this particular recipe?**

It's incredible. Every time people ask about that, even my father really doesn't know. Because he was a pastry chef in Naples and at the time that was one of the most important harbors in the Mediterranean, so he was able to get botanicals from South America from the Middle East and he actually tried to create probably 100 recipes. Originally he tried starting with a vermouth, but due to logistics problems he switched to the amaro because it was actually easier to produce and to stock. But he was really precise.

# COFFEE NEGRONI

LUCANO
5, VIA CAV. PASQUALE VENA, PISTICCI,
MT 75015, ITALY

While the name should conjure your typical Negroni (gin, sweet vermouth, and Campari), this Coffee Negroni from Lucano is anything but typical. For this drink, you use vodka instead of gin, amaretto in place of vermouth, and Cordial Caffè Lucano Anniversario in place of the Campari. The mix will have a nutty, sweet taste and a creamy texture.

※

**GLASSWARE:** Rocks glass

- **1 oz. Cordial Caffè Lucano Anniversario**
- **⅔ oz. Adriatico Amaretto**
- **1 ⅓ oz. vodka**
- **⅓ oz. vanilla syrup**

1. Fill a rocks glass with ice.

2. Add all the ingredients to a mixing glass with ice and stir.

3. Strain the cocktail into a rocks glass.

# EA SENSATION

LUCANO
5, VIA CAV. PASQUALE VENA, PISTICCI, MT 75015,
ITALY

Lucano's EA Sensation is a fun and simple cocktail to make. It combines the bittersweetness of their classic amaro with the smokiness of mezcal and the sweet aromatic notes from the vanilla liqueur. Fans of the Old Fashioned might find this oddly familiar (mixing a spirit with a sweet and bitter component), though the differences certainly outweigh the similarities.

---

✳

**GLASSWARE:** Rocks glass

**GARNISH:** Orange slice

---

- 1 ⅓ oz. Amaro Lucano
- 1 oz. mezcal
- ⅔ oz. vanilla liqueur

1. Add ice to a rocks glass.

2. Add the Amaro Lucano, mezcal, and vanilla liqueur to a mixing glass and stir.

3. Strain the cocktail into the rocks glass.

4. Garnish with a slice of orange.

# LIQUORE STREGA

PIAZZA VITTORIA COLONNA, 8, 82100 BENEVENTO BN, ITALY

Liquore Strega was first produced in 1860 by Giuseppe Alberti in the town of Benevento, located in the Campania region of southern Italy. The glowing yellow liqueur is one of the most unique products in Italy because it stands alone as both a singular product and a singular category of product.

*Strega* means "witch" in Italian, and this saffron-based liqueur combines dozens and dozens of other herbs and spices to achieve its one-of-a-kind flavor.

For cocktails, Strega is incredibly versatile and goes well with everything from mint and ginger to sour fruit juices and hazelnut liqueurs. There are many Strega recipes in this book that are all worth trying.

To get a better understanding of the liqueur's unique composition and history, I chatted with Strega CEO Giuseppe D'Avino about everything from the legend of the Benevento witches to the reason Strega shouldn't be grouped with any other liqueur.

### Let's start with some Strega history.

Strega was created by my great ancestor Giuseppe Alberti and he was a botanist. At that time, all the spices were used for medicine. Since he had this knowledge, he started to make up some liqueur recipes. At the very beginning of the business, they were mainly traders of wine, because the province of Benevento is the most important for grapes in the Campania region, and still is. Then he shifted from wine trading to the liqueur business. He developed Liquore Strega out of botanicals, quit the wine business, and focused on spirits. After him, the company was run by his children and grandchildren and so on, up to me and my cousin, which is the sixth generation.

Since it was a very typical Italian liqueur in the twentieth century, it also followed migrants from Italy to the rest of the world, because the twentieth century was a time of big emigration from Italy, especially to North and South America. This bottle was traveling with them and because of that, Liquore Strega became an internationally recognized product.

Also, in the bar sector they know what Strega is, which is a very specific product where the product itself is its own category. We are not like a bitter or amaro or sambuca, Strega is at the same time a product and a category. So, this is quite a mixed blessing because on one side you have to support the whole category. On the other hand, if someone wants your product, they have to take your product.

### What is the legend of the Benevento Witches?

They decided to name it "Strega" because of the legend of the Benevento witches. It's a very evocative name. It's something that sticks in your mind. It was fortunate that he decided to use this name for this product; the origin of the name was linked to the fact that Benevento is known, like Salem, [as] a place of witches.

### What is the legend of the witches?

The legend says that in Benevento the witches used to come from all over the world to meet for their witches' congress. The capital city of Benevento was the capital of the southern Italian kingdom of Langobards [a Germanic tribe that had come into the peninsula in the early Middle Ages]. And because the Langobards had totally different habits from the local population, they looked at these habits as something very strange, like magic, so maybe this is the reason why the legend was born.

# DICIOTTO 60

LIQUORE STREGA
PIAZZA VITTORIA COLONNA, 8, 82100 BENEVENTO BN,
ITALY

*D*iciotto means "eighteen" in Italian, and the name, combined with the number 60, pays homage to Liquore Strega's founding in 1860. Created by bartender Alex Frezza (see page 388), the drink itself is sweet, minty, fruity, and tart, and is a great celebration cocktail or ideal as a morning mimosa replacement.

✳

**GLASSWARE: Champagne goblet**

**GARNISH: Pink grapefruit zest**

- 1 oz. Liquore Strega
- 1 oz. pink grapefruit juice
- 2 dashes Angostura bitters
- 1 ⅔ oz. Champagne

1. Fill a shaker with ice and add Liquore Strega, grapefruit juice, and Angostura bitters.

2. Shake and strain the mixture into a champagne goblet.

3. Fill the goblet with the champagne.

4. Garnish with grapefruit zest.

# FIVE O'CLOCK

LIQUORE STREGA
PIAZZA VITTORIA COLONNA, 8, 82100 BENEVENTO BN,
ITALY

If there was an alcoholic drink to cure a cold, this would be it. When built on ice, this Alex Frezza concoction is both refreshing and sweet with hints of tartness and mint from the lemon juice and Strega. But when served hot (see the tip), it's the kind of tea that one can imagine drinking while cozying up in a giant blanket with a great book while it's snowing outside. It will cure whatever ails you.

---

✳

**GLASSWARE:** Collins glass

**GARNISH:** Eucalyptus sprig

---

- 3 oz. black tea
- 1 oz. eucalyptus honey
- 1 oz. Liquore Strega
- 1 oz. gin
- ⅔ oz. lemon juice

1. Prepare the tea. While it's hot, melt the honey inside.

2. Fill a shaker with the tea and the other ingredients, add ice, and shake vigorously.

3. Strain the drink into a collins glass filled with ice.

4. Garnish with a sprig of eucalyptus.

## TIP FROM ALEX FREZZA

This cocktail is also excellent hot. You can prepare it without having to shake, adding the ingredients directly to the hot tea one at a time. In this case, you can also enrich the garnish with a cinnamon stick or a slice of orange with cloves inside.

# FERNET-BRANCA

## VIA BROLETTO 35, 20121 MILANO MI, ITALY

Founded in 1845 in Milan by Bernardino Branca, the Fratelli Branca company started small, but word spread quickly and by 1907, there were factories in Buenos Aires, St. Louis, Switzerland, and New York.

The secret ingredient is held by the Branca family and includes cinchona, rhubarb, chamomile, cinnamon, linden, iris, saffron, galingale, myrrh, and many others that you'll simply have to guess at.

When it comes to cocktails, Fernet-Branca is beloved by bartenders (though they typically love it straight). In fact, Fernet-Branca created an entire marketing strategy around this love. In the bartender community, there's something known as the "bartender handshake." This is a practice for when bartenders are changing shifts and offer a shot of Fernet-Branca to the new mixologist on duty to mark the moment.

I was able to interview the president and CEO of Branca International, Niccolò Branca, to get a little more history and insight about the company. Afterwards, enjoy the recipes on the following pages.

### Can you please tell me about yourself and your family?

Under my leadership, our family business is now in its fifth generation. My family, starting with Bernardino Branca, the progenitor and founder of the company 178 years ago, has handed down from father to son the management and care of our company. Our company motto, "Novare serbando" (from Latin: "to innovate from tradition") sums up the way in which we look at the present, as well as the future.

### Can you describe how Fernet-Branca is made?

Born in 1845, initially as a medical remedy against digestive problems, Fernet-Branca has maintained over time the personality and originality with which it has conquered the five continents. Twenty-seven herbs, roots, and spices are the base that gives our liquid its typical brown color. These herbs come from four continents: Rhubarb from China,

Gentian from France, Galanga from India or Sri Lanka, Chamomile from Europe or Argentina, to name but a few. These herbs, roots, and spices are infused in alcohol, extracted or decocted. After one year, during which the blend has rested in oak barrels, evolving and blossoming all the aromatic components, the production process is complete. This long journey gives the brand its unique taste.

### How closely guarded is the recipe?

I'm currently the only person who holds the secret of the Fernet-Branca recipe. In fact, on arrival at the factory, the herbs for processing are manually tipped into the vats to avoid having to note down the quantities of the various ingredients.

### How has the current cocktail culture affected the company?

We have noticed a great openness on the part of contemporary cocktail culture to the world of bitters. Cocktails based on bitters represent a creative challenge for bartenders and an increasingly popular proposition for lovers of mixed drinks. It is perfect for all kinds of cocktails, from the simplest and most accessible such as the Fernet Mule, to more complex and sophisticated flavors such as the Brancamilano (see page 146).

# BRANCAMILANO

FERNET-BRANCA
VIA BROLETTO 35, 20121 MILANO MI, ITALY

A sweet vermouth, a super bitter liqueur, and a very old brandy (*stravecchio* means "aged") meet in Milan and come together to form a superb cocktail. Taking the three main products of the Branca brand, this mix is sweet, bitter, and herbaceous, and serves as a delightful aperitif. Try pairing it with salty appetizers, as the contrast of flavors will titillate your taste buds.

※

**GLASSWARE:** Old-fashioned glass

**GARNISH:** Peppermint leaves

- **2 oz. Carpano Antica Formula Vermouth**
- **½ oz. Fernet-Branca**
- **½ oz. Stravecchio Branca**

1. Fill a mixing glass with ice.

2. Add all the ingredients and stir.

3. Strain the cocktail into an old-fashioned glass.

4. Garnish with peppermint leaves.

# FERNET CUP N.1

FERNET-BRANCA
VIA BROLETTO 35, 20121 MILANO MI, ITALY

This cocktail is Fernet-Branca's take on a Moscow Mule. Replacing the vodka is the Fernet itself, while adding a little more sweetness with sugar syrup instead of just the standard ginger beer. If you really want to froth up this spicy, bittersweet concoction, add egg whites to the mix. It'll make the drink creamier without really changing the flavor profile.

---

✳

**GLASSWARE:** Moscow Mule mug
**GARNISH:** Lime wedge, mint leaves

---

- 1 ½ oz. Fernet-Branca
- ⅔ oz. sugar syrup
- ⅔ oz. lime juice

- ⅔ oz. egg whites (optional)
- Ginger beer, to top

1. Add ice to a Moscow Mule mug.

2. Add the Fernet-Branca, sugar syrup, and lime juice (and egg whites, if using) to a cocktail shaker with ice and shake vigorously.

3. Strain the mixture into the mug.

4. Top off with ginger beer.

5. Garnish with a lime wedge and mint leaves.

# POLI

VIA MARCONI 46, 36060 SCHIAVON (VI) - ITALIA

Founded in 1898 in Schiavon, near Bassano del Grappa, in the heart of Veneto, Italy, Poli Distillery is one of the oldest grappa houses in the world. The Poli family is still in charge here and the company still makes their grappa using ancient copper pots (with some modern additions like an innovative vacuum bain-marie).

Grappa is an acquired taste, as traditionally it was made by families without a high level of sophistication. Grappa is the product of distilling the grape skins, pulp, and seeds (pomace) that are left over from winemaking and it takes a high level of skill and well-refined equipment to achieve the smooth, often floral, and slightly sweet flavors.

Not until recently (think fifty years or so) have bartenders shown interest in using grappa to make cocktails. But Poli has made a concerted effort to work with the bartending community to use their products in a wide variety of concoctions. The Ve.N.To. cocktail (see page 154), in fact, is the first grappa-based drink to be included in the official 2020 IBA list of New Era Drinks.

As a distillery, Poli has also branched out into other distillates and liqueurs and today makes a line of vermouth, gin, whiskey, and a range of grappas with unique infusions like licorice, blueberry, and others.

Try out some of the inventive cocktails on the following pages and fall in love with Poli grappa.

# SARPARITA

POLI

VIA MARCONI 46, 36060 SCHIAVON VI, ITALY

Here's how Poli describes this twist on the classic Margarita: "Even though tequila and grappa express totally different aromas, they have in common a 'strong' personality, strictly linked to the land they come from. Sarpa Oro and UvaViva, with strawberry grape, are the protagonists of this variation of the classic Margarita, enriched with structure, aroma, and that rough harmony that makes this drink mysteriously attractive." You can't argue with mysteriously attractive, as this drink surprises in more ways than one.

**GLASSWARE:** Coupe glass (Mamo), chilled

**GARNISH:** Orange peel

- 1 ⅔ oz. Sarpa Oro Grappa
- ⅔ oz. fresh lime juice
- ⅔ oz. triple sec
- 2 barspoons liquid sugar
- 2 barspoons UvaViva Rossa Grape Brandy

1. Add all the ingredients to a cocktail shaker with ice and shake vigorously.

2. Strain the cocktail into a chilled coupe glass.

3. Garnish with an orange peel.

# VE.N.TO

POLI
VIA MARCONI 46, 36060 SCHIAVON VI, ITALY

The first grappa-based cocktail to be added to the official cocktail list kept by the International Bartender Association (IBA), the Ve.N.To was created by Samuele Ambrosi and Leonardo Varesi. The word *vento* in Italian means "wind," and Ambrosi said it was meant to evoke something that you can't touch but which unites everyone. The way the word is broken up is meant to symbolize the Veneto region and the Trentino-Alto Adige region—Ve.N.To. The cocktail itself will have a mixed profile, sweet with a chamomile flavor, floral from the grappa, acidic and tart from the lemon, and creamy from the egg white. It's a worthy addition to the IBA list and one you'll love making at home.

**GLASSWARE:** Tumbler glass

**GARNISH:** Lemon zest, white grapes

- 1 ½ oz. Poli Cleopatra Moscato Grappa
- ¾ oz. fresh lemon juice
- ½ oz. chamomile liqueur
- ½ oz. Honey Syrup (see recipe)
- ⅓ oz. egg white (optional)

1. Fill a short tumbler with ice.

2. Add all the ingredients to a cocktail shaker with ice and shake vigorously.

3. Strain the cocktail into the tumbler.

4. Garnish with lemon zest and three or four white grapes.

## HONEY SYRUP

On a stovetop, place a saucepan on low to medium heat. Add 1 cup water (or water with chamomile tea) and 1 cup honey and stir until combined. Let the mixture cool then bottle it. Use it immediately or store it in the refrigerator.

# AMARO MONTENEGRO

## VIA ENRICO FERMI, 4, 40069 ZOLA PREDOSA BO, ITALY

Amaro Montenegro is one of the most famous amaro's in the world. Created in 1885 by Stanislao Cobianchi in Bologna, Italy, the perfectly balanced liqueur is a digestif that is neither too sweet nor too bitter.

The name of the liqueur can be traced to a royal wedding. Originally, Amaro Montenegro was called Elisir Lungavita (Elixir of Life), but when Princess Elena of Montenegro married Prince Victor Emmanuel III, Cobianchi used the occasion to change the name to Amaro Montenegro.

The bottle itself is also unique, and as a chemist, Cobianchi wanted the look of it to resemble a vial where one might find valuable elixirs. The iconic shape has morphed a bit over time, but it's still unique enough to instantly spot in the back shelves of any bar around the world.

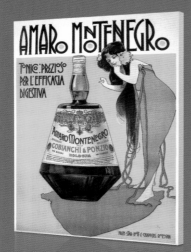

For a little more on the famous amaro, I talked to Gruppo Montenegro brand ambassador Rudi Carraro who explains what makes Amaro Montenegro special. After reading, head over to the next few pages for some iconic amaro cocktail recipes.

### Can you give me a little more color on Amaro Montenegro?

The founder, Stanislao Cobianchi, was a world traveler. He did a very good job of creating the liqueur which is still a model today after 137 years. Amaro Montenegro is the only amaro or one of the few that you can find from the very top north to the very deep south of Italy. So, it links Italy altogether. It's also an amaro that you can find in three Michelin star restaurants and in five-star luxury hotels. At the same time, you will find it in a very small bar in the last village in the middle of nowhere, in Sardinia. There is no F&B outlet in Italy that doesn't have a bottle of Amaro Montenegro. We still are the number one premium amaro in Italy. And we're very, very proud of that.

What makes Amaro Montenegro special in my point of view is the fact that it's very approachable, especially for non-Italian palates. And at the same time, it's also very versatile, because you can really, really create amazing cocktails. Also, simple recipes are great with Amaro Montenegro for example Amaro Montenegro and tonic water is very simple, and is a very delicious drink. At the same time, if you mix it up enough with Mezcal you have a "getting the party started cocktail" (see page 158). You can do a twist on a Manhattan with it (see page 160), you can twist a Negroni with it (see page 227). You can also cook with it. When I was in London, a chef friend of mine made Amaro Montenegro risotto and it was delicious. So, this is the beauty of it. Because we  always say that you need to be a master bartender to make a very good cocktail with the other amari. But you can just be an okay bartender to make cocktails with Amaro Montenegro.

# MONTE & MEZCAL

AMARO MONTENEGRO
VIA ENRICO FERMI, 4, 40069 ZOLA PREDOSA BO, ITALY

A maro Montenegro is bitter, herbal, and slightly sweet. Mezcal is typically earthy and smoky. Combine them together over ice and you have a marriage that is smooth and complex with notes that run the gamut of leathery to spicy to bitter to smoky.

✳

**GLASSWARE:** Low tumbler glass
**GARNISH:** Lime twist

- **2 oz. Amaro Montenegro**
- **2 oz. mezcal**

**1.** Fill a tumbler with ice, preferably one large cube.

**2.** Pour the amaro and mezcal into the tumbler and stir to mix.

**3.** Garnish with a lime twist.

# MONTE MANHATTAN

AMARO MONTENEGRO
VIA ENRICO FERMI, 4, 40069 ZOLA PREDOSA BO, ITALY

Taking a small spin on the most classic of cocktails, the Monte Manhattan replaces the typical sweet vermouth with the smooth, lightly bittersweet Amaro Montenegro. The result is a Manhattan with a little more bitterness but packing the same whiskey punch.

**GLASSWARE:** Coupe glass
**GARNISH:** Maraschino cherry

- 1 ½ oz. Amaro Montenegro
- 1 ½ oz. rye or bourbon whiskey
- 3 drops Angostura bitters

1. Fill a mixing glass with ice and then add all the ingredients.

2. Stir until well chilled.

3. Strain the cocktail into a coupe.

4. Garnish with a maraschino cherry.

# AVERNA

## CALTANISSETTA, SICILY

Averna Amaro is a traditional Italian liqueur from Sicily that has been around for nearly 150 years. To this day, the secret recipe is closely guarded, and it was originally created in the early nineteenth century by the Benedictine monks of Abbazia Di Santo. The monks allegedly gifted the secret to textile merchant Salvatore Averna for all the work he had been doing in the local community.

Salvatore Averna mostly made the amaro for his family and it wasn't until the late 1800s when the secret was passed to his son Francesco that it become more of a commercial product.

The tide truly turned for the Averna family when in 1895, King Umberto I gifted Francesco a golden brooch with the Savoy House emblem as a status symbol for the brand. And then in 1912, Vittorio Emanuele III gave Averna the right to place "Royal Household Patent" on the bottle.

Because it's so well guarded, the only known ingredients in Averna are Sicilian bitter orange and lemon essential oils, and pomegranate which give Averna a smooth taste and unmistakable aroma. But like most amari, there are likely upwards of 30 herbs and spices that make the blend so unique.

In the cocktail world, the signature drink that Averna is most associated with is the Black Manhattan (see page 94), which is a mix of amaro, rye, and Angostura Bitters. Averna is typically drunk as a digestif, but you'll find plenty of uses for this classic amaro for before or after dinner on the following pages.

Today, Averna is part of the Campari family of brands, and continues to be recognized as one of the best amaro's in the world.

# LIMONATA

AVERNA
CALTANISSETTA, SICILY

The sage aromas from this drink are probably its biggest selling point. But mostly, it's a very refreshing digestif that combines the mild bittersweet Averna with tart lemon juice and sweet simple syrup. Some fizz from the soda water ties it together. This feels like a Southern porch drink for watching fireflies dance in the summer night sky.

---

✳

**GLASSWARE:** Highball glass

**GARNISH:** Fresh sage leaf

---

- 2 oz. Amaro Averna
- 1 oz. lemon juice
- ¾ oz. sage-infused simple syrup
- 3 oz. soda water

1. Add ice to a highball.
2. Add all the ingredients, except the soda water, to a cocktail shaker with ice and shake vigorously.
3. Strain the mixture into the highball.
4. Top with the soda water.
5. Garnish with a sage leaf.

# MIDNIGHT TO MIDNIGHT

AVERNA
CALTANISSETTA, SICILY

Created by Seattle Bartender Adam Aly, the Midnight to Midnight is a classy-looking drink that hides a fusion of sweet and sour flavors beneath a thin layer of froth. The Amaro Averna is a sweet amaro, so this drink will lean on the sugary side, but the lime juice and pineapple juice will play a nice counter. Altogether, it's a very balanced cocktail that can help you wind down a late summer evening.

✳

**GLASSWARE:** Coupe glass, chilled

**GARNISH:** Lemon wheel

- 1 ½ oz. Amaro Averna
- ¼ oz. grenadine
- 1 oz. fresh pineapple juice
- 3 to 4 dashes cherry bitters
- ¾ oz. lime juice

1. Add all the ingredients to a shaker with ice and shake to chill.

2. Strain the cocktail into a chilled coupe with a fine mesh strainer.

3. Garnish with a lemon wheel.

# COCCHI

Cocchi was founded in 1891 by Giulio Cocchi and is well-known for their top-rated vermouths and for being one of the first companies to bottle a cocktail—namely the Americano, which is a vermouth with the addition of an alcoholic bitter.

Cocchi was also a prominent ingredient in an array of Futurist cocktails (see page 79), cocktails created during the 1920s and 1930s that were part of a cultural upheaval riding through Italy at the time. The cultural movement was particularly interested in new technologies and modernity and rejected old forms of art and culture.

I was able to talk to Roberto Bava who is the managing director of Cocchi to get a little more insight into the brand and its history.

### Can you walk me through the history of Cocchi?

We were born in 1891 and the company has been run by only two families in 132 years. One family was the family Cocchi, and the second family is Bava. I belong to the second family, which took over the business from the Cocchi family forty-five years ago. The story for us is that Giulio Cocchi was a real bartender. At the time we're calling this a barista if you prefer. And we discovered where he was working. The bar is still there and it's called Scudieri in Florence, which is one of the oldest bars in Florence. He decided to move to Torino because he wanted to make his own vermouth or his own wine, we don't know the story exactly. But we know how it came to be in Asti. He made a mistake. Instead of leaving the train in Torino, he got off the train one stop before which was in Asti, and he got lost at the station. To make it short, he finds someone to help him, and this guy had a bar in the main square in Asti. And he ends up marrying the daughter of this man, and the bar since then is still there and it's called Bar Cocchi. So, he wanted to make his own vermouth like many barmen, and he came to the right place because Asti is where things happen because Torino it's a town, but Asti is the agricultural wine province of Piemonte between Alba and Torino.

He started to create things and he's considered one of the founding fathers of Barolo Chinato. And he also bottled what could have been a cocktail or a modification of a cocktail called Aperitivo Americano. And his bottle was one of the first bottled Americano's where it was a vermouth with a drop of bitter in the American way. I wasn't there and it's difficult to know because I have been reading all of these facts coming out from old groups etc. But I am sure that his Americano outlived all the other ones.

Then they opened the distillery and the sparkling company. Cocchi still is fifty percent producing sparkling wines. In sparkling wine, Cocchi is a legend. We are kind of surprised to be, let's say, so famous around the world. So, we believe to be the new kid on the block for sparkling wine with 131 years of history. We are vintners, we are not a distiller and aromatized wine has a link with grapes, so anything wine with herbs in any way is a wine that we will make. So, you won't see a Cocchi gin, a Cocchi whiskey, etc. Every product of Cocchi is linked to grapes. It's a philosophy where we want to be the best aromatized wine producer in the world. That's it.

# ROSA ROSITA

COCCHI
ASTI, ITALY

The Rosa Rosita is like a beautiful marriage between a Mexican and an Italian. The Cocchi Rosa is a sweet vermouth with lots of herbal and fruity notes. Combined with a smooth white tequila and bitter Campari, this balanced drink comes out sweet, bitter, and a little spicy. It's a great aperitif on the hottest of days.

※

**GLASSWARE:** Rocks glass

**GARNISH:** Pink grapefruit peel

- 1 ½ oz. tequila blanco
- 1 oz. Cocchi Rosa
- ½ oz. Campari
- 2 dashes Angostura bitters

1. Fill a rocks glass with ice.
2. Add all the ingredients to a mixing glass with ice and stir for 15 to 20 seconds.
3. Strain the cocktail into the rocks glass.
4. Garnish with a pink grapefruit peel.

# EXTRA SONIC

## COCCHI
## ASTI, ITALY

Fans of dry and bitter cocktails will enjoy this one. The extra dry vermouth from Cocchi is a favorite among bartenders, especially for Martinis. For this cocktail, the vermouth is juiced up with double bubbles from the soda and tonic and a touch of anise from the absinthe. It's a clear, effervescent, and refreshing drink.

※

**GLASSWARE:** Collins glass

**GARNISH:** Mint sprig

- 2 oz. Cocchi Vermouth di Torino Extra Dry
- 3 drops absinthe blanche

- 2 oz. soda water
- 2 oz. tonic water

1. Fill a collins glass with ice.

2. Add the vermouth and absinthe.

3. Top with soda and tonic and stir gently.

4. Garnish with a mint sprig.

# PALLINI

Chances are you've seen the label. The Pallini Limoncello is easily the most recognized of every limoncello brand on the market. But Pallini is a company that goes back to 1875 and limoncello was not their first product.

Pallini's flagship is actually Mistrà, a liqueur made from seven types of aniseed, and is used in everything from cooking cakes and biscuits to enhancing espresso and of course, for cocktails. In addition to Mistrà, the company makes an excellent amaro, one of the best sambuca's on the market, their ubiquitous limoncello, and more.

You'll find multiple Pallini recipes in the next few pages, but I wanted to get the full story, so I talked to the company's CEO, Micaela Pallini, for history and more.

### Can you tell me a bit about Pallini, the company, you, and your family?

Pallini is a family-owned company based in Rome established in 1875 by Nicola Pallini. Nicola was actually a merchant more than a distiller or liquor producer. He established himself when he was quite young, in the small city of Antrodoco, which is in the center of Italy. And there, he opened the beginning of the Antica Casa Pallini, where he had the women of the area producing liqueurs for him. Sambuca is originally from Lazio, which is the region where we are and the area where we come from. So, in 1922, my great grandfather came to Rome, and transferred to Rome, and he realized the opportunities that a larger city could offer more than a small village like Antrodoco, so he transferred to Rome, and he was in the city center near the Pantheon. And we were there until the 1960s, and then it was where we started producing Mistrà, which is a dry anise.

**Can you talk about how the company went from this small town to becoming a global brand?**

The company went through several phases. One phase when he moved from Antrodoco to Rome. The second phase is when we started producing a brand called Romana Sambuca that was in the 1950s and 1960s. At the time, my father was working for Italian television and he was working in New York. And there he met a distributor. When he saw the bottle, he didn't know what Sambuca was, and then he tried it and he liked the concept, the label with the Colosseum, and the name. So, he called up his cousin and his brother and says, "You now order a container of the stuff and I will tell you how to sell it." At that time, there were only like five or six Italian liqueurs in the US like Amaretto Disaronno, Frangelico, Galliano, and Romana Sambuca. Many Americans never traveled out of the country until I would say the late 1980s; most Americans didn't even have a passport. At that time, the whole story, the idea of Rome, the Colosseum, the Dolce Vita and everything like this worked very well and the brand became the leading Sambuca in the United States.

**Are you seeing an uptick in interest for your products and Italian products in general?**

Around 2010 or 2015 mixologists became much more interested in what they were putting on the taste of the drinks. Italians like to use their hands, so they're good chefs, good mechanics, good bartenders, good at making stuff. It's kind of in our nature. A lot of young Italian kids went out and became famous bartenders. I think the era of Negroni really put a lot of things in motion. And then the bigger brands, which were tiny compared to some of the US multinationals, started working on it, and this is how the resurrection of the cocktails came about with Italian products.

# AROMA

PALLINI
VIA TIBURTINA, 1314, 00131 ROMA RM, ITALY

There's an old classic cocktail called a Hemingway Tonic made with grapefruit juice, gin, and tonic. The Aroma plays off the legendary writer's cocktail by replacing the gin with Pallini Limoncello. The grapefruit/lemon mix is both sweet and very tart, but the addition of Angostura bitters helps take the strength of that combo down a tad. It's an invigorating pre-dinner cocktail that's almost healthy.

※

**GLASSWARE:** Old-fashioned glass
**GARNISH:** Mint

- 2 oz. Pallini Limoncello
- 1 oz. grapefruit juice
- 2 to 3 dashes Angostura bitters
- 3 oz. tonic water

1. Add ice to an old-fashioned glass.

2. Add the limoncello, grapefruit juice, and Angostura to a mixing glass with ice and stir.

3. Strain the mixture into an old-fashioned glass.

4. Top with tonic water.

5. Garnish with mint.

# SLIPPERY NIPPLE

PALLINI
VIA TIBURTINA, 1314, 00131 ROMA RM, ITALY

The name alone is meant to get the party started, and this shot was made for exactly that. The Slippery Nipple is evocative, sweet, and sexy, and not in name only. The drop of grenadine at the bottom of the shot glass should form a little button that's supposed to look like a nipple (this only works with a thick syrup, so you can replace grenadine with something thicker if this part of the ritual is important to you). After you take the shot, you're meant to lick the nipple at the bottom. Have fun, kids!

✳

**GLASSWARE:** Shot glass

- ¼ oz. grenadine
- ⅔ oz. Sambuca Romana
- ⅔ oz. Bailey's Irish Cream Liqueur

**1.** Layering the ingredients slowly and carefully, first add the grenadine.

**2.** Then add the Sambuca Romana.

**3.** Finally, add the Bailey's.

# FORMIDABILE NEGRONI

PALLINI
VIA TIBURTINA, 1314, 00131 ROMA RM, ITALY

**P**allini doesn't only make limoncello; in fact they have a wide range of products including sambuca, a maraschino liqueur, and a number of amari. For this Negroni offshoot, you'll be using the company's Amaro Formidabile in place of the traditional Campari. It's a really unique liqueur that doesn't use any dyes or additives and lends the drink the right amount of bitterness to make this Negroni special and unique.

**GLASSWARE:** Rocks glass

**GARNISH:** Orange or lime slice

- 1 oz. Amaro Formidabile
- 1 oz. sweet vermouth
- 1 oz. gin

1. Add ice to a rocks glass.

2. Add all the ingredients to a mixing glass with ice and stir for about 30 seconds.

3. Strain the cocktail into the rocks glass.

4. Garnish with an orange slice or lime slice.

# VECCHIA ROMAGNA

VIA ENRICO FERMI, 4, 40069 ZOLA PREDOSA
BOLOGNA, ITALY

The story of Vecchia Romagna has its roots in France in the 1700s, but it's not until the fall of Napoleon that the Buton Family decided to move to Italy where the bounty of Italian grapes met up with a master distiller.

In 1820, Jean Buton set up an experimental distillery in Bologna, which led to the first Italian steam distillery in 1830. From this, Buton began making cognac that was celebrated all over the world.

Cut to 100 years later, and the company finally decided to embrace its Italian home by renaming the product Vecchia Romagna Buton Brandy and unveiled the first of their iconic triangular bottles with a laughing image of Bacchus on the front.

WWII nearly put the company under when bombing destroyed the distillery, but luckily, the underground cellar survived, and the company was able to rebuild on the backs of the barrels that were still holding their precious cargo.

Today, the company is owned by Gruppo Montenegro (Amaro Montenegro—see page 156 and Select Aperitivo—see page 224) and continues to make some of the finest brandy in the world. Vecchia Romagna has also become an ever-popular cocktail ingredient that enhances any post-dinner drinking hour.

Great on its own, neat or on the rocks, Vecchia Romagna has an unforgettable flavor that I'm sure you'll love when you make any of the recipes on the following pages.

# ORPHIC FLOWERS

VECCHIA ROMAGNA
VIA ENRICO FERMI, 4, 40069 ZOLA PREDOSA
BOLOGNA, ITALY

If you want to class up a cocktail party, the Orphic Flowers will do the job nicely. Served in a champagne coupe, the stunning, amber-colored drink mixes the smoothness of Vecchia Romagna brandy with the well-balanced combo of sugar and bitterness. When you top it off with champagne, the drink becomes lighter and more effervescent and can be used for any type of celebration.

**GLASSWARE:** Champagne coupe

**GARNISH:** Spruce essence, edible flowers

- 1 sugar cube
- 2 dashes Angostura bitters
- 1 ⅔ oz. Vecchia Romagna Tre Botti
- Champagne, to top

1. Soak the sugar cube with Angostura bitters and place the cube into a champagne coupe.

2. Add the Vecchia Romagna to a mixing glass with ice and stir until it is chilled and diluted.

3. Strain the drink into the coupe with the sugar cube.

4. Top off with champagne.

5. Garnish with spruce essence and edible flowers.

# THE RAIN NYMPH

VECCHIA ROMAGNA
VIA ENRICO FERMI, 4, 40069 ZOLA PREDOSA
BOLOGNA, ITALY

A very simple drink with a multilayered and complex flavor, The Rain Nymph takes the top-of-the-line Vecchia Romagna Etichetta and throws it together with patchouli syrup and lemon juice. The resulting mix is a medley of flavors that bounce from cinnamon and vanilla to earthy and tart. With each sip, you'll get a touch of sweetness from the sugar-rimmed glass that brings it all together. It's a beautifully simple yet sophisticated cocktail that will go down smoothly after dinner.

※

**GLASSWARE:** Nick & Nora glass

- **Sugar, for the rim**
- **1 ⅔ oz. Vecchia Romagna Etichetta Nera**
- **⅔ oz. lemon juice**
- **⅓ oz. patchouli syrup**

1. Rim a Nick & Nora with sugar.

2. Add all the ingredients to a cocktail shaker with ice and shake vigorously.

3. Double-strain into the Nick & Nora.

# LUXARDO

## VIA ROMANA 42, 35038 TORREGLIA—PADOVA PD, ITALY

Luxardo is an Italian liqueur brand that has been in operation since the early 1800s. The brand was founded by Girolamo Luxardo, who was a consul in Zara (now in modern-day Croatia) representing the Kingdom of Sardinia. Luxardo was interested in perfecting Rosolio Maraschino, which was a liqueur that was mostly produced in convents in the area since Medieval times.

In 1821, Luxardo established a distillery where he specialized in producing liqueurs made from maraschino cherries, a fruit that is native to the region around Zara. The maraschino liqueur was so popular that it became a favorite of royalty and nobility across Europe and Luxardo even obtained an exclusive license from the Emperor of Austria to make it specifically for him.

In the early 1900s, the company expanded its operations to include other fruit-based liqueurs such as limoncello, amaretto, and a popular cherry liqueur. During WWII, the company was nearly destroyed, but surviving members of the family managed to escape to Italy and restart from scratch.

Today, Luxardo is still owned and operated by the Luxardo family who have managed to maintain the brand's reputation for producing some of the finest liqueurs in the world that bartenders have always used and loved to make a wide array of cocktails—you can see many of them on the following pages.

For some added context, I went one-on-one with Matteo Luxardo, who is part of the sixth generation of Luxardo's to run the company:

**I'm curious as to why the family wanted to make the Rosolio Maraschino in the first place?**

Girolamo Luxardo's wife, Maria Canevari, found the recipe of the Rosolio Maraschino (the recipe was invented by a pharmacist in the beginning of the 1700s) and decide to produce it at home, as it was used those days by housewives. Girolamo saw that there could be a business behind that elixir, so he refined the recipe and in 1821 they started the company.

**What makes Luxardo unique/different?**

We are very different from the other Maraschino. First of all, it takes four years for the production; we harvest the cherries in late June, beginning of July, then we make an infusion with the solid part of the cherries, leaves, and branches of the marasca tree into alcohol for three years. After the infusion we distill everything, and then we put the distillate to rest in vats for another year. This is the secret.

# SOUR CHERRY MARTINEZ

LUXARDO

VIA ROMANA 42, 35038 TORREGLIA—PADOVA PD, ITALY

It's not 100 percent known who created the Martinez cocktail or even when it was first introduced, but scant evidence points to either bartender Jerry Thomas, or bartender Julio Richelieu, who lived in the town of Martinez, California. Poor records from the late 1800s aside, the cocktail originally called for gin, vermouth, bitters, and two dashes of Luxardo Maraschino Originale. Taking the drink into the twenty-first century, Luxardo mixed it up by using their Sour Cherry Gin to give the cocktail a little more tang. It's a precursor to a Martini, but it's sweeter and more bitter—if you're into that sort of thing (which you should be).

**GLASSWARE:** Coupe glass

**GARNISH:** Lemon zest

- 1 ½ oz. Luxardo Sour Cherry Gin
- 1 oz. sweet vermouth
- ¼ oz. Luxardo Maraschino Originale
- 2 dashes Angostura bitters

1. Fill a mixing glass with ice.

2. Add all of the ingredients to the mixing glass and stir.

3. Strain the cocktail into a coupe glass.

4. Garnish with lemon zest.

# IMPROVED LAST WORD

LUXARDO

VIA ROMANA 42, 35038 TORREGLIA—PADOVA PD, ITALY

The original Last Word cocktail dates to 1915 at the Detroit Athletic Club. But it was nearly lost to time until famed bartender Murray Stenson found its recipe in an old cocktail book in 2003. The recipe called for Luxardo Maraschino Originale, gin, green Chartreuse, and fresh lime juice. Luxardo decided it was time to improve upon the old classic and replaced the Chartreuse with its own Luxardo Liquore Sant'Antonio. It's a journey in your mouth with balancing flavors of bitter, sweet, and tart, with a crisp dry gin finish. Make this drink at home to impress your friends—it's a lime green stunner with a high level of sophistication when served in a coupe.

**GLASSWARE:** Coupe glass

**GARNISH:** Maraschino cherry

- 1 oz. Luxardo London Dry Gin
- 1 oz. Luxardo Liquore Sant'Antonio
- 1 oz. fresh lime juice
- ½ oz. Luxardo Maraschino Originale

**1.** Add all the ingredients to a shaker with ice and shake vigorously.

**2.** Double-strain the cocktail into a coupe.

**3.** Garnish with a maraschino cherry.

# MAROLO

DISTILLERIA SANTA TERESA, FRATELLI MAROLO S.R.L., CORSO CANALE 105/1, ALBA CN, ITALY

Grappa has been around for hundreds of years and was always considered a peasant drink, made from the waste products (skins, pulp, seeds, and stems) of grapes after they were pressed for making wine. But slowly, some companies popped up, realizing they could turn this "waste" into something special.

Though they're not the first, Marolo Grappa is special because they use single varietal grapes for their grappa and have been producing the stuff since 1977. Founded by Paolo Marolo and now run by Paolo and his son Lorenzo, Marolo produces one of the world's best grappas but they also make amaro, vermouth, and flavored wines.

Traditionally, grappa was never used as an ingredient for cocktails, but in more recent years, bartenders have been experimenting more and more, and incredibly complex and original cocktails using grappa have come about. You can find some Marolo-based recipes on the following pages.

For a little more about the company, here's Lorenzo Marolo on the history of this incredible brand.

### Tell me about the company.

Our distillery is a very young distillery because my father started in 1977. And everything, by the way, started as a hobby. He was studying at the Oenological School of Alba, where you study how to make wines, how to manage the vineyards, and so on. Then, he studied biology at the university, and he became a science professor. He had, at a certain point, the opportunity to teach the subject of making liqueurs, and it was a practical subject. So, they were buying certain products on the market, for example, Campari, and they were tasting the product and trying to repeat exactly the same recipe. It was that moment when my father fell in love with alcohol. And he said, okay, I'm in Alba, friends with a lot of winemakers, close to a very fresh raw material, so let me try to make a little bit of grappa myself. He started in the garage of my grandparents. My father from 1977 to 1991 was a teacher making a little bit of grappa. Let's say that the most important rule for my father is that in our life, we don't need to be lucky we just need to not be unlucky. So, in 1991, he was making enough bottles to survive on just his passion and at that point he quit the school to focus his attention on just making our products. The name of the distillery by the way is Distilleria Santa Teresa from Marolo. Why? Because as my father was starting into the garage of my grandparents, my grandparents at the time they were retired, and they bought a big house in the countryside here in Piemonte. That house was once owned by the church and nuns were living there and were devoted to Santa Teresa d'Ávila. So, when my father was figuring out what to call the product, he said nobody knows the name Marolo, so instead I'll use the name Santa Teresa and hopefully it will give me a little bit of luck.

MAROLO

GRAPPA DI MOSCATO
DISTILLATA A BAGNOMARIA
ALBA - ITALIA

42% vol.

# SCHÜMLI PFLÜMLI

MAROLO
DISTILLERIA SANTA TERESA, FRATELLI MAROLO S.R.L.
CORSO CANALE 105/1, ALBA CN, ITALY

Mixologist Stefano Giorgio Haegi created this elaborate cocktail at Herz in Basel, Switzerland, but it feels like it was invented in a lab. The drink is a dance of flavors and textures. Make sure to really shake this up so the egg white can help create a foam. Flavor-wise, you should expect a little sweetness, a little sourness, a little earthiness, and a fruity, chocolate-laced finish.

**GLASSWARE:** Highball glass

- 1 ⅓ oz. plum cordial
- ⅔ oz. Grappa di Moscato Marolo
- ⅔ oz. Bacalhôa Moscatel DOC Setúbal
- 1/5 oz. sour
- 3 drops dark chocolate
- ½ egg white
- Soda water, to top

1. Fill a highball with ice.

2. Fill a shaker with ice and add all the ingredients, except the soda water, and shake vigorously.

3. Strain the mixture into the highball.

4. Carefully add soda a little at a time until there's a nice head of foam on top.

# HEARTS AND DAGGERS

MAROLO
DISTILLERIA SANTA TERESA
FRATELLI MAROLO S.R.L. CORSO CANALE 105/1, ALBA
CN, ITALY

Created by mixologist Amie Ward when working at Aggio Restaurant in Baltimore, Maryland, the Hearts and Daggers cocktail is very sweet and floral. Marolo's Camomile Grappa has chamomile notes while the Chinato has a bit of spice. The strawberry syrup and lemon juice add a sugary and tart finish that is incredibly satisfying.

---

✳

---

**GLASSWARE:** Martini glass, chilled

**GARNISH:** Dehydrated cherry, fresh mint

---

- 1 ½ oz. Marolo Milla Camomile Grappa Liqueur
- 1 oz. strawberry syrup
- ½ oz. Marolo Barolo Chinato
- ½ oz. lemon juice

**1.** Add all the ingredients to a shaker with ice and shake vigorously.

**2.** Double-strain into a chilled martini glass.

**3.** Garnish with fresh mint and a dehydrated cherry.

# IL PIEMONTESE

MAROLO

DISTILLERIA SANTA TERESA, FRATELLI MAROLO S.R.L.

CORSO CANALE 105/1, ALBA CN, ITALY

A Negroni by another name, Il Piemontese was created by mixologist Adriano Volpe at Bar Les Trois Rois in Basel, Switzerland. Replacing your standard gin with Grappa di Barolo Bussia Riserva gives the drink some floral and spice notes that your average gin doesn't provide. Topping things off with a touch of white truffle essence gives the cocktail an undeniable aroma that will truly trick your brain and stomach into thinking it's time to eat.

---

✳

**GLASSWARE:** Coupe glass

**GARNISH:** Orange peel

---

- 1 oz. Grappa di Barolo Bussia Riserva "Marolo"
- 1 oz. Campari

- 1 oz. Vermouth di Torino Superiore "Umberto", D.co Ulrich
- 1 dash white truffle essence

1. Add all the ingredients to a mixing glass with ice and stir.

2. Strain the cocktail into a coupe.

3. Garnish with an orange peel.

# CINZANO

## VENETO, ITALY

Cinzano is a brand of vermouths and sparkling wines that have been in some form of production for over 260 years. Originating in Piedmont, Italy, the brand is known around the world thanks in part to the endless determination of its founders, brothers Giovanni Giacomo and Carlo Stefano Cinzano.

The Cinzano brothers founded Casa Cinzano in 1757, which was originally a confectionary specializing in transforming and preserving different types of fruit. But they also were experimenting with vermouth and the Cinzano name soon became synonymous with high-quality products. Over the years, the company developed a range of products including Cinzano sparkling wines, which come in dry, sweet, and rosé bottles. One of Cinzano's most notable creations is the Cuvée Storica, inspired by the brand's heritage and taking a cue from the King of Italy to create an Italian sparkling wine to rival champagne—it does a serviceable job at that.

As far as cocktails go, Cinzano has an equally long history and is recognized as the vermouth of choice for classic drinks like the Negroni (see page 29), The Americano (see page 30), the Cardinale (see page 65), and the famous Negroni Sbagliato (see page 57).

In 1999, Campari acquired the company and brought it into their ever-growing fold of legendary Italian liquor brands.

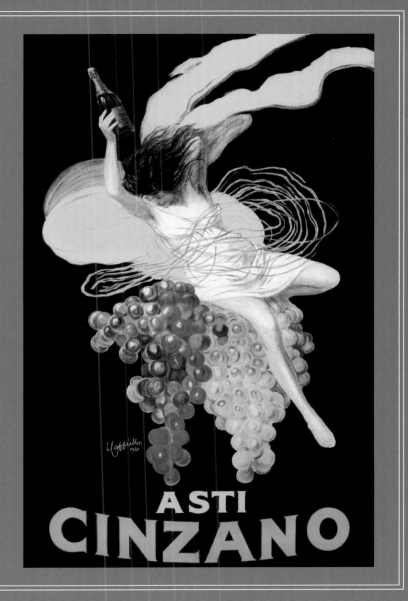

# CINZANO LA NUOVA TORINO

CINZANO
VENETO, ITALY

The Cinzano La Nuova Torino is a beautiful and sophisticated cocktail. The extra dry vermouth has a touch of bitterness and it pairs nicely with the whiskey—in particular the Glen Grant because of its smoother, smokier profile. The addition of chamomile honey and salt play well off each other and make this cocktail incredibly well rounded. Cocktail dresses and ties should be worn while sipping on this drink—that's what this level of sophistication calls for.

**GLASSWARE:** Manhattan glass (Cinzano uses Atelier Crestani Alchemica), chilled

**GARNISH:** Lemon zest

- 1 oz. Cinzano 1757 Vermouth di Torino G.I. Extra Dry
- 1 oz. Glen Grant 10-year Whisky
- 1 ½ barspoons chamomile honey
- 1 pinch pink Himalayan salt

1. Add all the ingredients to a cocktail shaker with ice and shake vigorously.
2. Double-strain the cocktail into a chilled Manhattan glass.
3. Garnish with lemon zest.

# ITALICUS ROSOLIO DI BERGAMOTTO

## AMALFI COAST, ITALY

While most Italian liqueur brands have hundreds of years of history under their belts, Italicus Rosolio di Bergamotto is practically brand new by comparison. Introduced in 2013, the bergamot-based liqueur hails from a UNESCO-protected area of Calabria where bergamot peels are macerated in alcohol and then combined with cedro from Sicily, Roman chamomile from Lazio, and Melissa balm (or lemon balm), lavender, yellow roses, and gentian from Northern Italy. It's a take on the historic Italian Rosolio—once considered the drink of kings, or *aperitivo di corte*.

This citrusy, yet slightly bitter concoction is the brainchild of Giuseppe Gallo, who was inspired by a recipe he found in a book that dates to the 1800s, *Il Liquorista Pratico*, by Luigi Sala. Gallo drew from family recipes that went back generations in the Amalfi Coast and was influenced by watching his mother make limoncello at home as a child. After years of experimentation, Italicus was born and quickly started garnering awards. In 2017, the liqueur won Best New Spirit of the Year at Tales of the Cocktail, Best Innovative Spirit at Bar Convent Berlin, and Double Gold at the San Francisco World Spirits Competition.

Today, Italicus is produced at a family-owned distillery, established in 1906 in Moncalieri, Torino, and is available all over the world. In 2022, the company signed a deal with Pernod Ricard in order to accelerate growth.

# MEZCALICUS

ITALICUS
AMALFI COAST, ITALY

With subtle nods to a Margarita and a Paloma, the Mezcalicus is a personal favorite of Italicus founder Giuseppe Gallo. Created by the awe-inspiring bartending team at Dead Rabbit in New York City, the drink melds the citrusy flavors of bergamot with the smokiness of mezcal. The splash of grapefruit juice gives it a nice tart kick at the finish.

---

✳

**GLASSWARE:** Coupette

**GARNISH:** Orange zest

---

- 1 oz. Italicus Rosolio di Bergamotto
- 1 oz. mezcal
- ¼ oz. fresh grapefruit juice

1. Pour all the ingredients into a shaker with ice and mix vigorously.

2. Strain the cocktail into a coupette.

3. Garnish with orange zest.

# ITALICUS CUP

R efreshing is typically the first adjective that comes to mind when you sip this idyllic aperitif cocktail. The flavors of Italicus are citrusy, with a touch of bitterness and a floral aroma, and when you combine it with the grapefruit soda, you achieve a subtle sweet essence with a pop of carbonation. Perfect for a pre-dinner drink, especially atop the cliffs of the Amalfi Coast where Italicus hails from.

✳

**GLASSWARE:** Highball glass

**GARNISH:** Grapefruit slice

- 1 ½ oz. grapefruit soda
- 1 oz. Italicus Rosolio di Bergamotto

**1.** Pour all the ingredients into the highball over ice cubes.

**2.** Garnish with a slice of grapefruit.

# DISARONNO

## SARONNO, ITALY

The story of Disaronno is hard to pin down. The history of the famous amaretto brand starts in 1525-ish during the Italian Renaissance. Legend has it that one of Leonardo da Vinci's pupils, Bernardino Luini, was paid to paint a fresco of the Madonna of the Miracles in Saronno (this fresco still exists today). Luini needed to find a muse to portray Madonna in the painting and he chose a local innkeeper. To thank him for the honor of being in his painting, the innkeeper gifted Luini a flask filled with a liqueur that was amber, fragrant, and delicious.

Sometime later, the founder of Disaronno, Domenico Reina, allegedly found this innkeeper and the secret recipe from the flask that was gifted to Luini. That secret has been passed down by every generation since and is still closely guarded to this day.

I talked to Simona Bianco, who is the Disaronno senior global marketing manager.

### Can you walk me through the legend of Disaronno?

I cannot tell you because I don't completely know, but we are 100 percent sure that this liquid has something to do with this legend of the painter and Madonna and this girl who was chosen as the Madonna. Because in Italy, especially in the little towns, families used to go to friends and use their own limoncello or liqueur as a gift especially during holiday season. So, this is what I can recall about the link between the legend and the story.

### Okay, so then let's jump ahead. When did Disaronno become the brand that we know of today?

In 1520 the Reina family had a little bodega in the center of Saronno, which was very typical, like a pharmacy, a place where you could go with your own bottle and fill it up. But then they started bottling in this beautiful Murano glass bottle, with these beautiful square caps, which have changed over the years, but the look and feel has always

been the same. The very first brand positioning for Amaretto Disaronno was as a gift. All the first advertisements, print advertising and
newspapers, were all positioning Disaronno as the perfect gift for the
holiday season.

**Are you seeing more Italian products, especially yours, being used
in cocktails?**

What I'm seeing all around the world is that many bartenders, especially Italian bartenders, of which there are many abroad, export the
heritage they have from their own country. Disaronno is a brand that
has been a part of very famous classic cocktails like the Godfather (see
page 76), the Amaretto Sour (see page 211), the French Connection.
And if you go on the top of the mixology pyramid, I would say that the
bartenders really enjoy the versatility of Disaronno, and I'm surprised
how they challenge themselves to get out of their comfort zones and
present something completely unexpected.

# DISARONNO SOUR

DISARONNO
SARONNO, ITALY

How many of these did you drink in college? The classic Amaretto Sour, or Disaronno Sour if you want to use the O.G., has always been an incredibly popular cocktail introduction to newly turned–21 American drinkers. And for good reason. This simple-to-make and incredibly tasty cocktail combines the sweetness of amaretto with the sourness of lemon juice in a perfectly proportioned way. Beginner or not, this drink is ideal for sipping on a hot summer day, lounging about after dinner, or, as the college kids like to do, pound in a club.

**GLASSWARE:** Rocks glass

**GARNISH:** Lemon slice

- 1 ⅔ oz. Disaronno Originale
- 4/5 oz. fresh lemon juice
- 1/6 oz. sugar syrup
- Egg white (optional)

1. Fill a rocks glass with ice.
2. Combine all the ingredients in a shaker with ice and shake vigorously.
3. Strain the cocktail into a rocks glass.
4. Garnish with a lemon slice.

# DISARONNO FIZZ

DISARONNO
SARONNO, ITALY

Y ou can definitely drink more than one. This low-ABV drink is a sweet and tart thirst-quencher that goes really well with a hot summer day. Think about this for a long, after-lunch drink on an open patio.

**GLASSWARE:** White wine glass
**GARNISH:** Lemon zest

- 1 ½ oz. Disaronno Originale
- 1 squeeze fresh lemon juice
- Club soda or sparkling water, to top

**1.** Pour the Disaronno Originale into a white wine glass with ice.

**2.** Add a squeeze of fresh lemon juice.

**3.** Top with club soda and stir.

**4.** Garnish with lemon zest.

# CYNAR

## PADUA, ITALY

In the very long list of amari, Cynar stands out for being a particularly bitter liqueur that's made with artichokes, herbs, and spices. The amaro was created in 1952 by Venetian entrepreneur Angelo Dalle Molle with the slogan "Cynar, against the stress of modern life."

Though the liqueur doesn't taste like artichokes, the name Cynar comes from a property found in artichokes called cynarin. It's believed that this property enhances the sweetness in other foods and drinks, and it's this, combined with thirteen different herbs and plants, that gives Cynar its unique flavor.

Now part of the Campari Group, Cynar has found a second life as a wonderful ingredient in cocktails. Traditionally, Cynar, like other amari is sipped neat or on the rocks after dinner. But in this book, you'll find a recipe for a Cynar Manhattan (see page 216), a Cynar Julep (see page 215), and a Cynar mixed with espresso for the ultimate digestif pick-me-up (see page 318).

# CYNAR JULEP

Cynar's version of a Mint Julep, this iteration replaces bourbon with Cynar to give the classic drink a bitter punch and a much lower ABV. To top it off and make it more refreshing, there's soda water for a carbonated effervescence. Remember, the more you muddle, the mintier the drink becomes.

* * *

**GLASSWARE:** Collins glass

**GARNISH:** Grapefruit slice, mint sprig

- 2 oz. Cynar
- ½ oz. simple syrup
- ½ oz. fresh lemon juice
- ½ oz. fresh grapefruit juice
- 12 mint leaves
- 2 oz. soda water
- 2 dashes Angostura bitters

1. In a collins glass, add Cynar, simple syrup, lemon juice, grapefruit juice, and mint and gently muddle.

2. Add ice and then soda water.

3. Top with dashes of bitters and stir.

4. Garnish with a slice of grapefruit and a sprig of mint.

# CYNAR MANHATTAN

## CYNAR
## PADUA, ITALY

The king of sophisticated drinks, the Manhattan has few equals. What's interesting about this Manhattan recipe is that it uses Cynar for its bitterness—and that bitterness will linger after each sip. Like your regular Manhattan, this elegant cocktail will have its reddish hues, but instead of a cherry garnish, this is cleaned up with a twist of lemon.

---

✳

**GLASSWARE:** Manhattan glass (Cynar uses Atelier Crestani Alchemica), chilled

**GARNISH:** Lemon twist

---

- 2 oz. Wild Turkey Whiskey
- ½ oz. Cynar
- ½ oz. Dolin Rouge Vermouth
- ½ oz. citrus simple syrup

1. Add all the ingredients to a mixing glass with ice and stir.

2. Strain the cocktail into the chilled Manhattan glass.

3. Garnish with a twist of lemon.

# BALDORIA

## BOVES, PROVINCE OF CUNEO, ITALY

Vermouth is a protected product (like most things in Italy), and to break through with something new and different can be painstaking and time consuming and usually not worth the effort.

But occasionally, something different comes along that reinvents the way we think about something we thought we already knew everything about.

That's where Baldoria comes in.

Created by renowned bartenders Timothée Prangé and Dotan Shalev (Experimental Cocktail Club and The Little Red Door in Paris), and entrepreneur Daniel Schmidt (CEO and COO of Ernest—the umbrella company that produces Baldoria), the vermouth brand is not only shaking up the old world of classic vermouths, it's riding a global trend where bartenders are demanding new and different vermouth products to spice up their cocktails.

Baldoria is the antithesis of Vermouth di Torino—the region where vermouth is typically made and where a consortium exists to protect its designation—and they're proud of that fact. I interviewed Baldoria CEO Daniel Schmidt about the brand and what they're doing differently. Check it out and then try some of the amazing cocktails on the following pages.

***Can you tell me about what you guys are doing?***

We're actually headquartered in California, but we live in Paris because it's a nice place to live, but our distillery is in Italy. It's actually in Piemonte, in the area of Cuneo in a small town called Boves. That's where most of our production takes place.

The main thing we're using is the Baldoria Vermouth, which is our vermouth. It's my favorite subject. We decided that we need to get involved in the production of spirits, because that's where the growth would come from. We looked at what we wanted to start with, and we decided vermouth was a very good starting point, for several reasons. The primary one is that vermouth is a product that nobody has really done anything with for the last 300 years that's really interesting or exciting. Since I think about 1780, or something, it's more or less the same, you have the red, the white, and the dry. If you look at what some of the brands are doing without mentioning them, they almost don't have real wine in them, in the sense that most of what's in them is synthetics and things like that. We decided we want to bring vermouth into the twenty-first century. We also thought that to be a twenty-first-century product, we need to move away from some of the bad habits that have gone into production and agriculture and begin to grow our own botanicals and our own wormwood and things like that.

So, we have a distillery in Boves, and there we have about ten acres of farmland where we grow most of our botanicals and we also have the legal rights to pick some of the botanicals from the hills of Piemonte, so it's based on Alpine botanicals and botanicals that we grow ourselves which are free of pesticides and fertilizers. And we use a very good wine in our various vermouths. We decided to start with the classic range, number one, out of respect for the product, but also to learn. We said we need to see how to create the classics and then move on. We set three parameters: We said number one, we want to be very different from what is known as Vermouth di Torino. When you look at Vermouth di Torino, they basically all taste the same, and we want to be different than that because there's just no sense in creating another vermouth that tastes the same as everything else. Number two, we wanted to create a product family where you can drink just the vermouth, you don't need to do anything other than put it in a tumbler with ice and enjoy it. And third, we wanted to create something where you can use it in both cooking and cocktails. And maybe a fourth thing, we said that while each one needs to be singular, there also has to be a connecting thread. So, you know, every product that we created in terms of tastes and sensations, they taste beautifully and delicious in a tumbler, and they can be used in cocktails, and they can be used in cooking in some of the best restaurants in France, Italy, the US and places like that.

# BALDORIA DRY & TONIC

BALDORIA
BOVES, PROVINCE OF CUNEO, ITALY

Baldoria's Dry Umami Vermouth is unlike any vermouth you've ever tasted. The umami in the name is apt as your palate memory searches its databanks and comes up with hints of mushrooms and seaweed. The vermouth itself is great for cooking, but for this simple recipe, it's just a refreshing way to start off a night. The effervescence of the tonic mixes nicely with the strangely enticing flavors of the vermouth and goes down very smoothly.

**GLASSWARE:** Highball glass

**GARNISH:** Cucumber slice

- 1 oz. Baldoria Dry Umami Vermouth
- 2 oz. tonic water

1. Place several ice cubes in a highball glass.

2. Add the vermouth.

3. Add the tonic water and gently stir.

4. Add a cucumber slice directly into the drink.

# DRY UMAMI SHERRY COBBLER

BALDORIA
BOVES, PROVINCE OF CUNEO, ITALY

The Baldoria team recommends drinking this cocktail with dinner—and when you consider its complexity of flavors, there are loads of options on the table. The sherry they use is both nutty and a bit salty, while the Baldoria Dry Umami Vermouth has a profile that includes porcini mushrooms and seaweed (heavy on the savoriness—hence umami). Mixed with a bit of lemon, this cocktail is a wow with a savory start, a salty middle, and a tangy and sour finish. Try it with risotto—and make that risotto with the same Baldoria Dry Umami—you'll be glad you did.

**GLASSWARE:** Highball glass
**GARNISH:** Lemon slice or basil sprig

- 4 oz. Amontillado Sherry
- 1 oz. lemon juice
- 2 oz. Baldoria Dry Umami Vermouth

1. Fill a highball with ice.

2. Add all the ingredients to a shaker with ice and shake vigorously.

3. Strain the cocktail into the highball.

4. Garnish with a slice of lemon or a sprig of basil.

# SELECT

## VENICE, ITALY

As I discussed in the aperitivo section of the book (see page 86), there are three different meanings to that word. Select Aperitivo is a bitter liqueur (not the happy hour or the category of drinks that fall under aperitifs).

Select was founded in Venice in 1920 and is often credited with being the first bitter liqueur combined with a Spritz and is the precursor to that entire milieu of drinks.

Back then, aperitifs were traditionally drunk neat or on the rocks (and still are), but today, the liqueurs are the bedrock for dozens and dozens of classic cocktails. Select can be used for Negronis, Americanos, Bicyclettes, and of course Spritzes.

Virtually any recipe in this book that calls for Aperol or Campari could be switched out with Select for a slightly changed flavor profile. It's absolutely worth experimenting with. You'll find some great recipes on the next few pages.

I talked to Select's Brand Ambassador Rudi Carraro who delves into the history of the brand.

### Can you start by comparing and contrasting Select with Aperol? Because I think a lot of people are confused by this?

Select was founded in Venice in 1920. If you look at Aperol, the bottle says 1919. This is the first debate that people have. Comparing Select to Aperol, their recipes are completely different. I'm not an Aperol expert in terms of their recipe because there is nothing that they disclose as far as what's inside. We can only guess that there might be oranges and some other botanicals. And they are 11 percent ABV, which is quite low. Whereas Select has thirty different botanicals, 17.5 percent ABV. I believe that our recipe is more complex than our competitors'.

When it comes to perception, our aim is to epitomize the offer of aperitivo out there. But at the same time, we have a very strong heritage and history. Nobody else can claim to be the original Venetian aperitivo from Venice, born in 1920. And you know, the one that set the trend. I'm not saying we were the first one or the last one, but we were the first one who said to try a Spritz with a bitter in it.

**Can you tell me about Select's history?**

Everything started in 1919, when the two Pilla brothers opened the distillery in downtown Venice. In the 1920s, they created Select. And this is just the product drunk neat with maybe a bit of ice. And they decided to invest in a marketing campaign which for that time was a little bit more advanced than what other companies were doing. They kept pushing until the brand had spread across the country. And the only problem during the journey of Select was the Second World War. Because the production in the 1930s was moved from downtown Venice to Porto Marghera Harbor, which is the main commercial hub in the mainland, close to Venice, and everything there was bombed and destroyed. So the two brothers found themselves with nothing. But this is the turning point, because they didn't give up, they moved to the island of Murano, which is very famous for glassblowing artists, and from there they continued with the production of Select and other products in the brand portfolio. Luckily for them, after the Second World War it was very prosperous times for Italy, so they slowly started to get back, first in the Venetian territory, and then a bit longer for the whole country, and then internationally after Gruppo Montenegro took over in 1988.

# SMOKE & BITTERS

The Smoke & Bitters is what it says it is—a smoky drink (thanks to the mezcal) and a bitter drink (thanks to the amaro and Select). It's a bit similar to a Mezcal Negroni replacing the sweet vermouth with amaro, but the taste is similar, if not a bit smoother, given Amaro Montenegro's perfectly balanced flavor.

✳

**GLASSWARE:** Rocks glass

**GARNISH:** Orange twist

- **1 oz. Select Aperitivo**
- **1 oz. mezcal**
- **1 oz. Amaro Montenegro**

**1.** Place a large ice cube in a rocks glass.

**2.** Combine all the ingredients in a mixing glass.

**3.** Add ice and stir for 30 seconds.

**4.** Strain the cocktail into the rocks glass over the ice.

**5.** Garnish with an orange twist.

# BROKEN BICYCLETTE

SELECT
VENICE, ITALY

Maybe a misnomer, this drink is more accurately described as an "enhanced" Bicyclette. The original Bicyclette recipe calls for dry white wine, Campari, and soda, mimicking a traditional Spritz but without the prosecco. The Select version, of course, replaces Campari with its own aperitivo and adds peach nectar. It's not only refreshing, but sweet and sparkling without being overbearing. It's a wonderful summer drink.

---

✳

**GLASSWARE:** Highball glass
**GARNISH:** Thyme sprig

---

- **3 oz. dry white wine**
- **1 oz. peach nectar**
- **2 oz. Select Aperitivo**
- **1 oz. soda water**

1. Pour the wine, peach nectar, and Select into a cocktail shaker with ice and shake.

2. Strain the mixture into a glass filled with ice.

3. Top with soda water and gently stir.

4. Garnish with a thyme sprig.

# ITALIAN HANDSHAKE

SELECT
VENICE, ITALY

Colloquially, a bartender's handshake is simply a shot (usually Fernet-Branca) from one practitioner to another—on the house—as a means of ingratiating yourself to a fellow tribesperson. Select's Italian Handshake takes this concept up a level by adding a shot of its Aperitivo to a beer. It's a simple drink, an easy drink, and any guest at home or at a bar will be pleasantly surprised at this no-nonsense welcome to a night out.

※

**GLASSWARE:** Pint glass, chilled

---

- **12 oz. chilled lager or pilsner**
- **2 oz. Select Aperitivo**

1. Pour the beer into the chilled pint glass.

2. Slowly pour the Select into the beer.

# FRANGELICO

## PIEDMONT, ITALY

Frangelico is a fascinating liqueur whose history dates back to the 1600s and Christian monks who were adept at the art of distilling, in particular with the hazelnuts found in the region. The name Frangelico is a portmanteau of Fra' Angelico, the name of a hermit friar who lived in the Piedmont hills back in the day. The monks are also the inspiration for the shape of the bottles—a Christian friar with a cord tied around his waist.

The liqueur itself is made from Italian hazelnuts that are toasted and infused in alcohol and water. The flavoring is enriched with a combination of cocoa seeds, vanilla, roasted coffee, and more. Because of its sweet nature, the liqueur can be added to a wide variety of cocktails, most of which make for excellent after-dinner drinks. But Frangelico can also be sipped on the rocks with a little bit of lime.

If you're looking for something sugary after a meal, but don't necessarily want/need the calories of a grandiose dessert, Frangelico is an excellent substitute—in fact there's even a recipe for a Cake Shot (see page 315) to completely satiate your sweet tooth.

# HAZELNUT OLD FASHIONED

FRANGELICO
PIEDMONT, ITALY

There are many ways to change up a classic Old Fashioned. The traditional recipe has just bourbon, sugar, and bitters. Frangelico's version doesn't deviate far from that mix either, but with the addition of their hazelnut liqueur, the cocktail takes on a whole new flavor profile—making it more of an Old Fashioned cousin than a sibling. Try it out—Frangelico is a fun way to spice up this old standby.

**GLASSWARE:** Rocks glass

**GARNISH:** Lemon peel

- 1 oz. Frangelico
- 1 oz. Wild Turkey 101 Bourbon
- ¼ oz. simple syrup
- 4 dashes aromatic bitters

**1.** Add a large ice cube to a rocks glass.

**2.** Add all the ingredients to a mixing glass with ice and stir.

**3.** Strain the cocktail into a rocks glass.

**4.** Garnish with a lemon peel.

# CLASSIC ITALIAN HOTEL BARS

PEACH BELLINI

VERUSCHKA

LEGACY

THE GORILLA

WATERMELON PALOMA

FRANCO'S FIZZ

SILK ROUTE

GRAND TOUR

INDIAN ROUTE

IL BORRO SOUR

NEGRONI AFRODITE

LA GRANDE BELLEZZA

NEGRONI BERGAMOTTO E BASILICO

SUNSET ZONE

BEVERLY INTERPRETATION

MI-VÀ

MILANESE CAIPIRINHA

MIRTO SPRITZ

QUEEN 56

For most of the nineteenth and twentieth centuries, serious cocktail drinking in Italy was a sophisticated affair, targeting well-heeled locals and tourists, and isolated almost entirely within the hallowed halls of glitzy five-star hotels.

These bars catered to classy drinkers who had experienced cocktailing in major cities like London, New York, and Paris. Throughout Italy, you could find an array of vintage spots that served everyone from royal families and Hollywood celebrities to CEOs, heads of governments, and more.

Some of the best hotels across Italy have been serving for 100+ years and are responsible for training nearly every great bartender in and out of the country today. Nowadays, the hotel bars are still some of the top places to drink, but the cocktails have become more adventurous and the mixologists more worldly.

Of course, you can still find perfect versions of classic drinks, but the dress codes are mostly gone, though the see-and-be-seen crowds remain.

In the following pages are some of Italy's most celebrated and historic hotel bars (with a few newer ones peppered in), and the cocktail virtuosos serving drinks that almost always come with timeless stories.

# HASSLER BAR

## PIAZZA DELLA TRINITÀ DEI MONTI, 6, 00187 ROMA RM, ITALY

Long before the modern cocktail culture became pervasive in Rome, it was the luxury hotels that provided well-off locals and upscale tourists with the best drinks in the city. The Hotel Hassler Roma is one of those hotels, iconic in that it sits at the top of the Spanish Steps and gives guests a true sense for the majesty of the Eternal City.

The hotel as it's known today was renovated and restored in 1947, but it's been operating and serving everyone from royal patrons to Hollywood movie stars since 1893. The hotel has welcomed the Kennedy's, Pablo Picasso, Justin Timberlake, and Princess Diana—who once confessed to the late Roberto E. Wirth (the former president and general manager of the Hassler) that the Peach Bellini they served at the Hassler was her favorite in the world (see page 240).

Today, the famous Hassler Bar is run by Stefano Santucci, who has been bartending for more than thirty-two years, with eighteen at the Hassler. Here's a one-on-one with the legendary Barman behind this legendary bar.

### What makes the Hassler Bar unique?

The Hassler Bar, a jewel box hidden in the back of the hotel's Salone Eva restaurant, is a cozy, hidden cocktail bar, ideal for an aperitif or an after-dinner drink. Decorated with dark wood, red-leather upholstery and gilded mirrors, it is like stepping back in time. Lounge on a leather sofa or sit at the bar and watch the bartenders carefully mix, muddle, and pour the rare bitters, liquors, and the various flavorsome ingredients to create unbeatable cocktails such us the famous Veruschka, (see page 243).

### How would you describe the cocktail culture in Rome?

Over the past few years, the cocktail world has had an impressive growth here. The new cocktail era is based on innovation and using new techniques, but always with a focus on the best quality ingredients.

Furthermore, the bar scene has completely changed. Wine/cocktails and food have always gone well together, and now it is becoming even more popular to explore the pairings of cocktails with different dishes. Pairing cocktails with food means that cocktails can be created and invented to match perfectly with a dish, like two "chefs" who work together to create a flavor experience.

# PEACH BELLINI

HASSLER BAR
PIAZZA DELLA TRINITÀ DEI MONTI, 6, 00187 ROMA RM,
ITALY

While the Bellini was invented by Giuseppe Cipriani at the famous Harry's Bar in Venice (see page 49), it's the Hassler Bar's version that has royal backing. This simple, refined, and sweet Bellini is so good that Princess Diana once confessed to the late Roberto E. Wirth, former president and general manager of the Hassler, that this particular Bellini was her favorite. To make it at the highest level takes a few days because the puree is the secret. But once it's done, this magical elixir will be a fan favorite amongst your friends.

**GLASSWARE:** Champagne flute

**GARNISH:** Slice of peach

- ⅔ oz. Peach Puree (see recipe)
- 3 ⅓ oz. prosecco

1. Pour the peach puree and prosecco into a mixing glass filled with ice and quickly stir.

2. Strain the cocktail directly into a champagne flute.

3. Garnish with a slice of peach.

## PEACH PUREE

Place four white peaches (washed, pitted, peeled, and sliced) into a large stainless steel bowl with 13 ½ oz. pinot grigio and two raspberries. After 3 days, remove the peaches and place them in an earthenware bowl and refrigerate them for a few hours. Then place the peaches, the juice of one lemon, 60 grams sugar, and the pinot grigio and blend until the puree is completely smooth.

# VERUSCHKA

HASSLER BAR
PIAZZA DELLA TRINITÀ DEI MONTI, 6, 00187 ROMA RM,
ITALY

Named after former hotel owner Roberto Wirth's daughter, this refreshing cocktail is made with pomegranates, prosecco, and a drop of vodka. The drink is light, has hints of sweetness and tartness from the pomegranates, and the prosecco tickles your throat on the way down. Its vibrant red color gives the cocktail a seductive quality and is a great opener to start off a date. The *purea di melograno fresca* is a fresh pomegranate puree. The hotel bar shells the pomegranates and squeezes the seeds to make it. You can also simply buy pomegranate puree as a substitute.

**GLASSWARE:** Champagne flute

**GARNISH:** Rose petal

- 1 ¼ oz. fresh pomegranate puree
- Splash vodka
- Prosecco, to top

1. Fill a champagne flute with the pomegranate puree.

2. Fill the rest of the glass with prosecco and top it off with a splash of vodka.

# ATRIUM BAR AT FOUR SEASONS HOTEL FIRENZE

## BORGO PINTI, 99, 50121 FIRENZE FI, ITALY

Built out of a fifteenth-century Medici palace, the Four Seasons in Florence is truly a one-of-a-kind hotel. The moment you walk in, you're confronted by a white marble nineteenth-century replica of the famous Bacchus statue by Michelangelo and bathed in sunlight from the skylights above.

It stands to reason that a hotel of this magnitude would have a bar to match, and the Atrium lives up to all expectations. Helmed by master mixologist and Florence-born Edoardo Sandri, the bar is famous for its advanced cocktails that incorporate everything from liquid nitrogen to oyster leaves. I had the chance to ask him a few questions about his style.

### Have you incorporated anything from Florence into your cocktail making?

I'm very passionate about local street culture. In 2019, I created a cocktail inspired by one of Florence's most iconic dishes, the Lampredotto, cow entrails best served in a sandwich on the street. We named the drink Negroni Completo, a typical Negroni with Lampredotto ingredients. The ultimate blend of local legends.

### How would you describe your bartending style?

I like to play, moving fast, using my physical strength. I like to compare my boxing style with my bartending methods. Every year we try to innovate and find new ways to improve ourselves with unexplored tools and techniques like aging, smoking, distillation, decomposition, thermal processes . . . we usually have a lot of fun indeed.

### Do you think about the history of Italian cocktails when you're making drinks?

Our traditional aperitivo and liqueurs style can be considered pioneering and inspired so many cultures all over the world. Personally, I prefer dry drinks, without too much sugar, sometimes easy, sometimes brainy techniques. I try to be rational with an emotional, unpredictable twist. Just like Italian people.

# LEGACY

This steely blue cocktail is simple to make but complex when it comes to flavor. Atrium's bartender Edoardo Sandri is a master at mixing aromas and flavors, and the butterfly tea plays a key role in adding floral essence with every sip. The Patrón is key because it's incredibly smooth, while the amber martini gives the drink its sweetness. This drink is a feast for the eyes, nose, and taste buds that works in perfect harmony.

✳

**GLASSWARE:** Caraiba tumbler

- 1 ⅓ oz. Patrón Silver
- 1 oz. butterfly tea
- ½ oz. amber martini
- ½ oz. lemon juice
- ⅓ oz. oleo clementine saccharum

1. Add all the ingredients to a shaker with ice.

2. Strain the cocktail into the Caraiba tumbler.

# THE GORILLA

ATRIUM BAR AT FOUR SEASONS HOTEL FIRENZE
BORGO PINTI, 99, 50121 FIRENZE FI, ITALY

When you order a drink at the Atrium Bar inside the stunning Four Seasons in Florence, you're always in for a show. Bartender Edoardo Sandri is a science wizard with a mix of infusions, smoky effects, and dizzying ingredients that are feasts for all the senses. The Gorilla is no exception. Tropical and smoky, this cocktail will delight your palate with sweetness and bitterness along with a refreshing carbonated kick. The not-too-much effort pays off in the end (but if you need to cheat, you can buy pineapple soda for a less-good version).

**GLASSWARE:** Porcelain mug
**GARNISH:** Dried cornflower

- 4/5 oz. Casamigos Mezcal
- 4/5 oz. Michter's Bourbon Whiskey
- 4/5 oz. Bitter Fusetti
- 1 ⅓ oz. Gorilla Mix (see recipe)

1. Fill a porcelain mug with ice.

2. Add the mezcal, bourbon, Bitter Fusetti, and Gorilla Mix to a shaker with ice and shake vigorously.

3. Strain the cocktail into the porcelain mug.

4. Garnish with dried cornflower.

# GORILLA MIX

Chill 24 oz. lapsang souchong tea in the refrigerator. While the tea is chilling, blend 150 grams fresh pineapple. Combine the pineapple, tea, and 3 ⅓ oz. coconut syrup and stir. Use a carbonation machine or soda siphon to carbonate the mixture.

# FRANCO'S BAR

## VIA CRISTOFORO COLOMBO, 30, 84017 POSITANO SA, ITALY

Possibly the most picturesque bar in the country, Franco's Bar in Positano on the Amalfi Coast has a perch that looks over the Tyrrhenian Sea and surrounding hills. Franco's is named after Franco Sersale, one of four siblings who founded Le Sirenuse in 1951, the hotel where Franco's resides. Everywhere you look, you'll find meticulous design elements and priceless works of art—and that's before you order a drink or soak in the view.

Cocktails here are served in stunning Venetian glassware that only adds to the drama of drinking in the perfect locale. Another unique feature is that the bar won't take reservations. You could be a member of a royal family or a Hollywood celebrity—many of whom have passed through—and you'll be treated like anyone else. It's the most beautiful egalitarian bar in the world.

Check out some of the recipes from the bar on the next few pages and for a little more insight, I interviewed Aldo Sersale, the son of current La Sirenuse/Franco's Bar owners Antonio and Carla Sersale:

**What makes Franco's unique? Obviously, the setting is one-of-a-kind, but what sets it apart from other bars in Positano?**

There are so many details that make Franco's Bar greater than the sum of its parts. The one-of-a-kind setting and breathtaking view are of course very important, but it's the design elements that create its unique atmosphere—Giuseppe Ducrot's imposing yellow ceramic fountain, a forty-year-old lemon tree, floor tiles by Fornace de Martino, graffiti by Karl Holmqvist, Venetian glassware, and beautiful furniture designed by Paolo Calcagni. An upbeat playlist, incredible cocktails, and great service help, too.

**What do you think of Italian cocktail culture? Have you noticed any changes to the way people drink since opening?**

Italian cocktail culture is in a renaissance, three bars—L'Antiquario in Naples (see page 388), Drink Kong in Rome (see page 330) and 1930 in Milan—have made it into the fifty best bar list for the first time. Italians are becoming more curious and discerning in terms of mixology—no longer will we only be known for Negronis and Aperol Spritz!

An interesting change we have noticed is the rise in popularity of mocktails made with non-alcoholic distillates such as Seedlip.

**What kinds of cocktails is Franco's making? What is it known for? Are there a lot of limoncello based drinks on the menu?**

Our cocktail list is divided into The Icons—our classics with a faithful following, The Twists—enduring favorites, refreshed and rebooted and The Lights—delicious, seductive, and alcohol-free. We have a wide variety of cocktail styles using different base spirits and we try to stay away from molecular mixology instead focusing on local ingredients, local spices, and premium spirits. Most of our cocktails are refreshing with some element of citrus as it's a summer venue.

Funnily enough we do not have a cocktail made with Limoncello on our list, but we do offer a wonderful Limoncello Spritz that we worked on for those who ask.

**How has Franco's changed or evolved over time?**

Franco's has become "the" place to be in Positano. Revered not only for its view, but for its incredible mixology. The service has become more informal, the ambiance more special, and the queue even longer!

# WATERMELON PALOMA

FRANCO'S BAR
VIA CRISTOFORO COLOMBO, 30, 84017 POSITANO SA,
ITALY

Franco's Bar doesn't completely reinvent the wheel on its version of a Paloma, but you could argue they make it much better than its classic counterpart. Substituting grapefruit juice with watermelon, this Paloma is much sweeter but still gets a nice tang from the lemon juice. It's as refreshing as it gets, and perfect for thinking about those sunset views in the mountains of the Amalfi Coast.

* * *

**GLASSWARE:** Collins glass (Franco's glass is made by Nude Glass)
**GARNISH:** Lemon zest

- Salt, for the rim
- 1 ⅔ oz. Casamigos Blanco Tequila
- ½ oz. agave syrup
- 1 ⅔ oz. fresh watermelon juice
- ½ oz. lemon juice

1. Salt the rim of a collins glass and add ice.
2. Add all the ingredients directly to the glass and stir.
3. Garnish with lemon zest.

# FRANCO'S FIZZ

FRANCO'S BAR
VIA CRISTOFORO COLOMBO, 30, 84017 POSITANO SA,
ITALY

Atypical Fizz is usually a mix of any kind of spirit along with sugar, citrus juice, and sparkling water. If you go to Franco's in Positano (and you should go for the views alone), their version brings almond milk into play, which not only makes the drink prettier, it smooths it out as well. They also use Italicus (see page 202), which is a liqueur that's made with the sour/citrus bergamot.

**GLASSWARE:** Collins glass (Franco's Fizz glass is made by Laguna~B)

**GARNISH:** Lemon zest

- **Ground pistachios mixed with salt, for the rim**
- **2 oz. almond milk**
- **1 ⅔ oz. Italicus**
- **½ oz. lemon juice**
- **1/6 oz. simple syrup**
- **1 ⅔ oz. lemon soda**

**1.** Wet the rim of a collins glass and dip it into the pistachios/salt mix.

**2.** Fill the glass with one or two ice cubes.

**3.** Add the almond milk, Italicus, and lemon juice to a shaker with ice and shake vigorously.

**4.** Strain the mixture into the collins glass and then add the soda water.

**5.** Garnish with lemon zest.

# JULEP HERBAL & VERMOUTH BAR AT HOTEL DE LA VILLE

## VIA SISTINA, 69, 00187 ROMA RM, ITALY

Hotel de la Ville is a luxurious 5-star hotel with a primo location at the top of the Spanish Steps in the heart of Rome. Today, Hotel de la Ville offers its guests luxurious accommodations, impeccable service, and breathtaking views of the Eternal City. It's steeped with history and remains one of Rome's most iconic hotels.

Inside the hotel is the Julep Herbal & Vermouth Bar, which has a one-of-a-kind cocktail program that's inspired by the thirteenth-century spice route that started in Venice and wended its way around Europe and Asia.

# SILK ROUTE

JULEP HERBAL & VERMOUTH BAR AT HOTEL
DE LA VILLE
VIA SISTINA, 69, 00187 ROMA RM, ITALY

The aesthetics of the Hotel de la Ville in Rome are dripping with sophistication and the cocktails fit into the same milieu. A visual masterpiece, the Silk Route is a cocktail that leans heavily into the ancient trading road that spanned across the European and Asian continents. The ingredients stretch geographic boundaries with cassia (cinnamon), Szechuan pepper, French vermouth, and Russian vodka, and scintillate and entice with every sip. Take a journey with this drink and sip slowly while you dream of the long lost past.

**GLASSWARE:** Coupette

**GARNISH:** Orange twist, angel's hair chili

- **Pinch cassia**
- **Pinch Szechuan pepper**
- **1 oz. Grey Goose Vodka**
- **1 oz. Noilly Prat Dry Vermouth**
- **⅓ oz. Rabarbaro Zucca**

1. Grind the Szechuan pepper and cassia using a mortar and pestle.

2. Add the cassia, pepper, and remaining ingredients to a mixing glass with ice and stir gently.

3. Double-strain the cocktail into a coupette.

4. Garnish with an orange twist wrapped around an angel's hair chili.

# GRAND TOUR

JULEP HERBAL & VERMOUTH BAR AT HOTEL
DE LA VILLE
VIA SISTINA, 69, 00187 ROMA RM, ITALY

Sweet, sour, and herbal, the Grand Tour cocktail from the team at Julep Herbal & Vermouth Bar in Rome found the perfect balance of flavors. The name "Grand Tour" is apt, as this drink brings in ingredients from Italy, Spain, and Russia. Overall, the profile will be refreshing, and if you sip subtly, the mint garnish will titillate your nostrils, further enhancing this stellar cocktail.

**GLASSWARE:** Mancino Alto glass, chilled

**GARNISH:** Roman mint

- 1 ½ oz. Stoli Elite Vodka
- ½ oz. lemon juice
- ½ oz. liquore alloro (bay leaf liqueur)
- ½ oz. sugar syrup
- ½ oz. Yzaguirre Blanco Vermouth
- Pinch Erba del Vescovo

1. Add all the ingredients to a shaker with ice and shake vigorously.

2. Double-strain into a chilled Mancino Alto glass.

3. Garnish with Roman mint.

# INDIAN ROUTE

JULEP HERBAL & VERMOUTH BAR AT HOTEL
DE LA VILLE
VIA SISTINA, 69, 00187 ROMA RM, ITALY

The team at the Julep Herbal & Vermouth Bar have themed their cocktails along the old Silk Road. And this adventurous concoction dabbles into India by using cardamom, turmeric, and tamarind spices throughout the drinking journey. This incredibly sophisticated cocktail will evolve with each sip—you'll experience sweetness and spiciness from the glass rim and dual rums, a hint of bittersweet from the Doppio Carvi, and some citrusy tang from the lime. If this doesn't transport you to India a thousand years ago, not much else will.

**GLASSWARE:** Mancino Alto glass

- **Green tea sugar, as needed, for the rim**
- **Cardamom, as needed, for the rim**
- **1 ⅓ oz. Blanc Blanc Rum**
- **⅔ oz. Doppio Carvi Liqueur**
- **½ oz. Appleton Estate Signature Blend Rum**
- **½ oz. lime juice**
- **⅓ oz. simple syrup**
- **1 barspoon tamarind syrup**
- **Small pinch turmeric**

**1.** Rim a Mancino Alto glass with green tea sugar and cardamom.

**2.** Add all the ingredients to a shaker with ice and shake vigorously.

**3.** Double-strain the cocktail into the Mancino Alto glass.

# TUSCAN BISTRO AT IL BORRO

## LUNGARNO DEGLI ACCIAIUOLI, 80R, 50123 FIRENZE FI, ITALY

Il Borro is a resort in the Tuscan countryside that's carved out of a thirteenth-century palace and opened by the esteemed Ferragamo family. Once you arrive, you're bathed in luxury, especially when it comes to the food, wine, and cocktails.

    The Tuscan Bistro is their flagship restaurant with locations around the world. But the one at Il Borro just feels better because you're in the heart of Tuscany, surrounded by vineyards, and the cocktails are simply the cherry on top of the experience.

# IL BORRO SOUR

TUSCAN BISTRO AT IL BORRO
LUNGARNO DEGLI ACCIAIUOLI, 80R, 50123 FIRENZE FI,
ITALY

For the perfect taste of Tuscany (and luxury), the Il Borro Sour from the stunning Ferragamo-owned Il Borro resort is a smooth and delicate cocktail that's ideal for a sunset sip. There are notes of citrus from the lemon juice, while the elderflower liqueur gives the drink more fragrance and a spicy sensation. The saline water adds a hint of salt, and the egg whites help froth up the drink. If you can't make it to Tuscany, this cocktail, created by bartender Francisco León, will bring it home to you. For the honey syrup, you can make your own at home (see page 155 for a recipe).

**GLASSWARE:** White wine glass

**GARNISH:** Grated Tuscan black pepper, rosemary sprig

- 1 ⅓ oz. Vodka VKA
- ⅔ oz. elderflower liqueur
- ½ oz. Il Borro honey syrup, flavored with rosemary
- ½ oz. lemon juice
- ⅓ oz. egg white
- 3 drops saline solution (see page 23)

1. Pour the vodka, elderflower liquer, honey syrup, lemon juice, and egg white into a dry shaker and dry-shake for 10 seconds.

2. Add ice to the shaker and shake more vigorously.

3. Pour all the contents of the shaker into a white wine glass without straining.

4. Garnish with grated black pepper and a rosemary sprig.

# STRAVINSKIJ BAR AT HOTEL DE RUSSIE

## VIA DEL BABUINO, 9, 00187 ROMA RM, ITALY

Hotel de Russie in Rome sits in a prime location between Piazza del Popolo and the magnificent Villa Borghese Park in the middle of the city. Famous guests range from the King of Sweden and Napoleon's brother to long stints by Pablo Picasso and Jean Cocteau. Cocteau is particularly noteworthy as he worked on *Parade*, the Cubist ballet with music by Igor Stravinsky—which leads us to the now famous Stravinskij Bar.

The bar itself has a stunning outdoor patio, surrounded by overhanging trees and colonnaded stairs and porticos. Helmed by master Bar Manager Paolo Dianini, the bar teems with life nearly every hour of the day and is home to an array of amazing cocktails. Here's a Q&A with the legendary barman.

### How does Italy, and Rome in particular, inspire your bartending?

There's so much history and culture in Italy and in Rome in particular, which drives my inspiration for our menu at Stravinskij Bar. Each region in Italy offers its own unique ingredients, flavors, and traditions which can be incorporated into cocktail creations.

For example, ancient Rome served as our inspiration to create Stravinskij Bar's seasonal beverage, Roma Antiqua, which is a simple yet refined cocktail that takes guests back in time, imagining Roman emperors imbibing and dining.

The Roma Antiqua cocktail is a nod to the abundance of grapes in ancient Rome, where they were a staple at banquets and events. The drink is made primarily from pressed white grapes and grape brandy and is garnished with a small bunch of grapes. To pay homage to the traditional pre-dinner drink of the Imperial Roman era, we add a touch of honey to the mix. To complete the authentic experience, we serve the Roma Antiqua in traditional amphora cups and metal glasses.

# NEGRONI AFRODITE

STRAVINSKIJ BAR AT HOTEL DE RUSSIE
VIA DEL BABUINO, 9, 00187 ROMA RM, ITALY

Paolo Dianini has been manning the Stravinskij Bar inside the tony Hotel de Russie since 2000 and has no shortage of interesting cocktails on his menu. One of the best is this offshoot of a Negroni. Instead of using a sweet vermouth, Dianini brings together Lillet Blanc and Tio Pepe Sherry to give this drink a nutty and savory flavor. The fresh strawberries are a nice touch to offset any bitterness and the large ice chunk will help keep dilution to a minimum.

**GLASSWARE:** Nick & Nora glass, chilled

**GARNISH:** Strawberries

- 1 oz. Martin Miller's Original Gin
- ⅓ oz. Campari
- ⅔ oz. Lillet Blanc
- ¼ oz. Tio Pepe Sherry

1. Add a large ice chunk to a chilled Nick & Nora.

2. Add all the ingredients to a mixing glass with ice and stir until well chilled.

3. Strain the cocktail into Nick & Nora glass.

4. Garnish with fresh strawberries.

# IL GIARDINO BAR

## HOTEL EDEN, VIA LUDOVISI, 49, 00187 ROMA RM, ITALY

The Hotel Eden in Rome officially opened in 1889 and was immediately considered one of the top hotels for elite guests visiting the Eternal City. The hotel's prime location finds it on the southwest corner of Villa Borghese Park and boasts stellar views of the city and five-star accommodations, dining, and of course drinking.

Il Giardino Bar has one of the best sunset perches in all of Rome, and it also has the drinks to match. Run by master mixologist Stefano Briganti, the menu features a long list of classic and signature cocktails that are aimed to wow, and they do exactly that. Cocktails here aren't cheap, but the view, the setting, and the flavors make it worth every euro.

# LA GRANDE BELLEZZA

IL GIARDINO BAR
HOTEL EDEN, VIA LUDOVISI, 49, 00187 ROMA RM, ITALY

Created by Stefano Briganti at the historic Il Giardino inside the Hotel Eden in Rome, La Grande Bellezza is a time-consuming concoction, but (fortunately) only the first time you make it. The key to the drink is infusing the tangy sweetness of tamarind into vermouth, which takes a few days. But once you have the bottle ready, you can impress your guests with this exquisite cocktail that combines tang with the smoothness of tequila and smokiness of mezcal. It's a showstopper.

**GLASSWARE:** Coupette

**GARNISH:** Edible flowers

- 2 oz. Tamarind-Infused Vermouth (see recipe)
- ¾ oz. Espolòn Blanco Tequila
- 1/6 oz. Mezcal Nuestra Soledad
- 2 drops mandarin bitters

**1.** Add all the ingredients to a mixing glass with ice.

**2.** Strain into a coupette with two ice cubes.

**3.** Garnish with edible flowers.

## TAMARIND-INFUSED VERMOUTH

Combine ½ cup tamarind paste and one bottle of Martini & Rossi Vermouth in a large jar. Seal the jar and shake well, then store it in a cool, dark place for 3 to 4 days. Strain the vermouth through a cheesecloth into a clean bottle and store the bottle in the refrigerator.

# NEGRONI BERGAMOTTO E BASILICO

IL GIARDINO BAR
HOTEL EDEN, VIA LUDOVISI, 49, 00187 ROMA RM, ITALY

A new take on the Negroni, bartender Stefano Briganti's version at the Il Giardino Ristorante balances the normal 1-1-1 ratio with a couple twists. A normal Negroni will have equal parts vermouth, gin, and Campari, but here, Briganti uses bergamot liqueur which adds an element of bitter citrus to the mix. The slightly muddled basil brings out a pepperiness and helps elevate this drink for a perfect summer-time start to any night.

**GLASSWARE:** Old-fashioned glass

**GARNISH:** Basil leaf, lemon peel

- 1 ½ oz. Campari
- 4/5 oz. Tanqueray London Dry Gin
- 4/5 oz. Quaglia Bergamot Liqueur
- ⅓ oz. Carpano Antica Formula Vermouth

1. Fill an old-fashioned glass with ice.

2. In a mixing glass, very lightly muddle two-thirds of a basil leaf.

3. Add all the ingredients and ice to the mixing glass.

4. Stir and strain the cocktail into the old-fashioned glass.

5. Garnish with the remaining basil and a lemon peel.

# BEVERLY AT THE HOXTON ROME

## LARGO BENEDETTO MARCELLO, 220, 00198 ROMA RM, ITALY

The Hoxton Rome is one of the newer hotels in the city, but its focus on a top-of-the-line cocktail program puts them in line with some of the best hotels in the city.

Like most Hoxtons around the world, the lobby is an inviting space where young professionals come to work, socialize, and of course, drink. There are two bars on the main floor, but the real action happens at the Beverly, the California-themed indoor/outdoor restaurant and bar that wants guests to forget the city outside and dream of the Pacific coastline.

The cocktails keep things light with lots of tropical options, but of course you can come by any classics here as well. At the head of the action is bartender Simone De Luca. De Luca hails from Naples, but like almost every great bartender in Italy, he learned his trade in London working at spots like the Punch Room in the London Edition, where his work garnered the bar a "Tales of the Cocktail" nomination as one of the four best hotel bars in the world.

# SUNSET ZONE

BEVERLY AT THE HOXTON ROME
LARGO BENEDETTO MARCELLO, 220, 00198 ROMA RM,
ITALY

A sunset zone is a gardening term that tells you where a plant will grow year-round. Bartender Simone De Luca at Beverly lovingly calls this drink the same name because it refers to areas where bananas can easily flourish. This sweet and fruity drink takes you right to the beaches of Southern California, as it not only tastes like a refreshing summer cocktail, but its color also resembles the perfect sunsets off the Pacific coastline.

**GLASSWARE:** Rocks glass
**GARNISH:** Banana chip

- 1 ⅔ oz. Woodford Reserve Bourbon
- ⅔ oz. banana liqueur
- 1/6 oz. Kahlúa
- 1/6 oz. demerara syrup
- 2 dashes orange bitters

1. Pour all the ingredients into a mixing glass with ice and stir.

2. Fill a rocks glass with a giant ice cube.

3. Strain the cocktail into the rocks glass.

4. Garnish with a banana chip.

# BEVERLY INTERPRETATION

BEVERLY AT THE HOXTON ROME
LARGO BENEDETTO MARCELLO, 220, 00198 ROMA RM,
ITALY

The Beverly Interpretation is bartender Simone De Luca's version of a classic Spritz. The "Interpretation" comes in using Italicus (a bergamot liqueur) as the citrusy alcohol base and carbonating the drink with chinotto, which adds notes of caramel and more citrus. To unsweeten things a tad, the pink grapefruit juice lends its tartness and balances this stunning cocktail out nicely.

---

✳

**GLASSWARE: Champagne glass**
**GARNISH: Green leaf**

---

- 1 ⅔ oz. Italicus
- ½ oz. fresh pink grapefruit juice
- 5 oz. Lurisia Chinotto

1. Pour all the ingredients into a mixing glass with ice and stir.

2. Strain the cocktail into the champagne glass.

3. Garnish with a green leaf.

# PRINCIPE BAR AT HOTEL PRINCIPE DI SAVOIA

## PIAZZA DELLA REPUBBLICA, 17, 20124 MILANO MI, ITALY

Principe di Savoia is an icon when it comes to luxury accommodation in Milan. The hotel opened its doors in 1927 and was quickly adopted by the crème de la crème of high society. Celebrity guests have included the Duke of Windsor, Charlie Chaplin, Josephine Baker, and Maria Callas. And the Principe Bar at the hotel has served some of the city's best cocktails to everyone from Madonna and Quentin Tarantino to George Clooney and Beyoncé.

The hotel and bar are hot spots during Milan's fashion weeks as highly skilled bartenders whip up signature Martini's, champagne cocktails, and old-school classics.

Today, the hotel is part of the Dorchester Collection, which includes other legendary spots like the Beverly Hills Hotel, Hôtel Plaza Athénée in Paris, and Hotel Eden in Rome (see page 274).

# MI-VÀ

The Hotel Principe di Savoia opened in 1927 in Milan and is a five-star spot that's home to a see-and-be-seen crowd, especially during Fashion Week. The Principe Bar lives up to the hotel's exalted reputation with a refined and unique drinks program. The Mi-Và fits right in with the runway crowd, as this ruby red showstopper gives its glitterati guests a sweet and sour drink that looks as good as it tastes. For your next bougie cocktail party, serve this drink to impress your fanciest friends. It pairs especially well with tempura prawns.

**GLASSWARE:** High Tumbler

**GARNISH:** Pink grapefruit slice

- 1 oz. Principe Gin
- 1 oz. Campari
- ⅓ oz. sweet-and-sour mix
- Grapefruit tonic, to top

**1.** Add a large ice chunk to a high tumbler glass.

**2.** In a mixing glass, stir the gin, Campari, and sweet-and-sour mix.

**3.** Pour into a high tumbler and then top with tonic.

**4.** Garnish with a slice of grapefruit.

# MILANESE CAIPIRINHA

PRINCIPE BAR AT HOTEL PRINCIPE DI SAVOIA
PIAZZA DELLA REPUBBLICA, 17, 20124 MILANO MI, ITALY

This is the Hotel Principe di Savoia's unique take on the classic Brazilian Caipirinha. The twist to this vintage drink is the addition of orange bitters and saffron powder—saffron being a particularly well-known spice in Milan and used in the sumptuous Risotto alla Milanese. Overall, this Caipirinha will be slightly more bitter and a little more floral than the original and radiate with a bright yellow glow because of the saffron.

**GLASSWARE:** Medium tumbler glass

**GARNISH:** Lime wedge

- ½ lime, cut into small pieces
- 2 teaspoons brown sugar
- 2 oz. cachaça
- Dash orange bitters
- Saffron powder, to top

1. Add the lime and sugar to a medium tumbler and muddle together until the sugar is dissolved.

2. Add crushed ice to the glass to about two-thirds full.

3. Pour the cachaça and a dash of orange bitters over the ice.

4. Gently stir to combine the ingredients.

5. Top with a sprinkle of saffron powder.

6. Garnish with a lime wedge.

# CONRAD CHIA LAGUNA SARDINIA

## VIALE DEI FENICOTTERI, 52, 09010 DOMUS DE MARIA SU, ITALY

Overlooking Chia Bay on the island of Sardinia, the Conrad Chia Laguna is a luxury resort with all the fixings. The secluded property rests on the southern tip of the island where sandy beaches meet pink flamingos and where wild herbs bless the air with the aromas of mint, rosemary, and thyme.

The Bollicine Bar is where the cocktail action takes place, and it leans in heavily on its name. *Bollicine* means "bubbles," and here there are loads of champagne, prosecco, and spumante-based cocktails to keep things light and playful.

Sardinia is also home to the myrtle plant, which is used in the island's homegrown liqueur, Mirto. Mirto is a fruity, slightly bitter concoction that lends itself to making a wide range of cocktails. Lucky for us, the hotel provided a couple recipes to get you into the Italian island spirit.

# MIRTO SPRITZ

CONRAD CHIA LAGUNA SARDINIA
VIALE DEI FENICOTTERI, 52, 09010 DOMUS DE MARIA
SU, ITALY

The original Spritz al Mirto was created by Maurizio Urru at the Balentes Café in Padova. That version used Campari to add an extra layer of bitter and color. The rendition at Chia Laguna is stripped down and only has Mirto, soda, and prosecco. Mirto is a myrtle berry liqueur that is local to Sardinia and often sipped on its own as a digestif. In cocktails, it takes on a new dimension, adding vibrant, fruity, and slightly bitter flavors. The Mirto Spritz is an aperitif that will make you dream of the soaring Sardinian cliffs crashing against the Tyrrhenian Sea.

**GLASSWARE:** White wine glass

**GARNISH:** Dehydrated orange

- ⅔ oz. mirto
- 2 oz. prosecco
- Soda water, to top

1. Fill a wine glass with ice.

2. Once the glass is chilled, toss the ice away.

3. Add the Mirto, then the prosecco, and top with soda water. Gently stir.

4. Garnish with a dehydrated orange slice.

# TIP

Add a bit more orange flavor by rimming the glass with the orange slice.

# QUEEN 56

REGINA ISABELLA BAR
PIAZZA SANTA RESTITUTA, 1, 80076 LACCO AMENO NA,
ITALY

The island of Ischia is off the west coast of Naples and is home to the stunning Regina Isabella Resort. The hotel has always been an A-list celebrity spot and many flock to the island paradise during the annual Ischia Film Festival. At the resort, bar manager Mariano Pezzella wows guests with a wide array of original cocktail creations, and one of his favorites is the Queen 56. According to Pezzella, "The cocktail is an anytime drink, but perfect for the classic Italian aperitivo and it's easy to replicate at home." Mainly the drink screams island life with a citrus hit that goes well with the celebratory nature of the prosecco.

**GLASSWARE:** Brandy snifter (or vintage cocktail glass)
**GARNISH:** Cinnamon stick, lemon peel, or mandarin peel

- 1 oz. gin
- 1 oz. Mandarin Liqueur (see recipe)
- ½ oz. lemon juice
- 2 oz. Prosecco D.O.C.G.

1. Add all the ingredients, except the prosecco, to a mixing glass and stir.

2. Strain the mixture into a snifter and top with the prosecco.

3. Garnish with a cinnamon stick, lemon peel, or mandarin peel.

# MANDARIN LIQUEUR

Peel 15 fresh mandarins and add them to a large jar. Top with 1 liter vodka (or other liquor) and seal the jar for 7 days. Combine 1 liter water and 800 grams sugar in a saucepan and heat until the sugar is dissolved. Let it cool. Strain the mandarin-infused vodka through a fine-mesh strainer and combine with the syrup. Mix well. Store the liqueur in a cool, dry place or in the freezer.

# DIGESTIVO:

# THE ART OF POST-DINNER DRINKING IN ITALY

AMARO SOUR

COPPOLA

STAZIONE STREGA

BIANCO STREGA

ESPRESSO LUCANO

TRIPLE PROPHECY

CAKE SHOT

FRANGELI-COCOA

CAFFE CORRETTO

VELVET WHITE ESPRESSO MARTINI

CAFFE SHAKERATO

SICILIAN ESPRESSO MARTINI

To drink like a true Italian, you have to understand the different breakdowns of the day. Before dinner, as discussed, is the aperitivo, a time to drink cocktails that stimulate the appetite and get you (and your stomach) in the mood to eat. Dinner is typically paired with wine and followed by dessert and coffee. But after coffee, Italians drink digestivi or digestifs, which are meant to help you settle your stomach and digest your food.

On digestif menus in Italy you'll usually find a wide range of amari, fernet, grappe, and other mostly bitter liqueurs. But you'll also discover a sweet side that includes amaretto, limoncello, sambuca, and more.

Now you might be wondering why digestifs and aperitifs have a lot of crossover, and you'd be right to ask that question. There's nothing scientific about the types of drinks the Italians have both before and after dinner, it's more about culture. But there is some evidence to suggest that bitter drinks can help on both sides of the meal.

Traditionally, digestifs are drunk neat or on the rocks. They are sipping liqueurs, meant to help you wind down. But this is a cocktail book, so we're going to look at the entire category of after-dinner drinks—some that will in fact wind you down, others to keep the evening flowing, and others to supercharge a night that's just about to explode.

There's no one way to drink after dinner, and the following cocktails will help you find the right one for you at the right time.

# AMARO SOUR

B ona Furtuna is a company that hails from Corleone, Italy (yes, the same place as in *The Godfather*), and is typically known for their award-winning olive oil. But the farm produces a bevy of products, among them an incredible line of honeys. For cocktail purposes, Bona Furtuna's Pine Honey mixes perfectly with the extra bitter Amaro Averna and fresh lemon juice to create a complex, bittersweet drink. The gin adds a crisp finish, but you can also make the Amaro Sour with bourbon for a smokier profile.

**GLASSWARE:** Rocks glass

**GARNISH:** Rosemary sprig

- 2 oz. gin or bourbon
- 1 oz. Amaro Averna
- 1 oz. fresh lemon juice
- 1 tablespoon Pine Honey Simple Syrup (see recipe)

1. Fill a rocks glass with ice.

2. Add all the ingredients to a shaker with ice and shake vigorously.

3. Strain the cocktail into the rocks glass.

4. Garnish with rosemary.

# PINE HONEY SIMPLE SYRUP

Add ¼ cup Bona Fortuna Pine Honey and ¼ cup water to a pan and simmer on the stovetop. Stir until the honey dissolves. Allow the syrup to cool completely before use.

# COPPOLA

Riding an oncoming Italian bar wave, the Capri Club in Los Angeles (see page 392) is one of the latest and greatest Italian cocktail bars in America and hosts loads of rare Italian liqueurs. The master bartenders are wizards with combinations and the Coppola is one great example. This cocktail is a hybrid of a Black Manhattan and a Sazerac. It's earthy, herbaceous, bitter, and has a little spice to it. This is a great winter drink that can be enjoyed after a meal.

---

✳

**GLASSWARE:** Stemmed rocks glass, chilled

**GARNISH:** Lemon peel

---

- Absinthe, to rinse
- 1 ½ oz. rye whiskey
- ½ oz. Averna Amaro

- ¼ oz. Brucato Chaparral
- 2 dashes orange bitters
- 2 dashes Angostura bitters

1. Spray a chilled stemmed rocks glass twice with an atomizer filled with absinthe.

2. In a mixing glass, add the rest of the ingredients and stir for 30 seconds.

3. Pour the cocktail into the rocks glass.

4. Express a lemon peel over the cocktail.

# STAZIONE STREGA

LIQUORE STREGA
PIAZZA VITTORIA COLONNA, 8, 82100 BENEVENTO BN,
ITALY

Liquore Strega and fernet are polar opposites. Strega is sweet and minty and fernet is powerfully bitter. Bartender Alex Frezza calls these two liqueurs the antagonists in this drink and then uses the red vermouth to balance everything out. The ruby color of the cocktail makes it feel classier than most and is a hit as both a pre-dinner aperitif and an after-dinner digestif—you can thank the antagonists for that duality.

---

✳

**GLASSWARE:** Nick & Nora glass, chilled

**GARNISH:** Orange zest

---

- **1 oz. Liquore Strega**
- **1 oz. Fernet-Branca**
- **1 oz. red vermouth**

1. Chill a mixing glass.

2. Pour all the ingredients into the mixing glass with ice and shake for 20 seconds.

3. Strain the cocktail into a chilled Nick & Nora.

4. Twist the orange peel to get the essential oils into the drink.

5. Rub the orange peel on the stem of the glass and discard.

# BIANCO STREGA

LIQUORE STREGA
PIAZZA VITTORIA COLONNA, 8, 82100 BENEVENTO BN,
ITALY

**B**artender Alex Frezza places this cocktail into a winter category of Strega drinks. The nutmeg and hazelnut scream Christmas and curling up by a fire. This is a great after-dinner drink that will pair perfectly with bites of rich, dark chocolate.

---

✳

**GLASSWARE:** Coupe glass, chilled

**GARNISH:** Nutmeg, orange peel

---

- 1 oz. Liquore Strega
- 1 oz. fresh cream
- ⅔ oz. spiced rum
- ⅔ oz. hazelnut liqueur
- ½ oz. water

1. Add all the ingredients to a shaker with ice and shake vigorously.

2. Strain into a chilled coupe glass.

3. Grate nutmeg on the surface of the drink.

4. Garnish with an orange peel.

# ESPRESSO LUCANO

LUCANO

5, VIA CAV. PASQUALE VENA, PISTICCI, MT 75015, ITALY

If you want an after-dinner pick-me-up, Lucano has the perfect drink for you. The Cordial Caffè Lucano Anniversario is a coffee liqueur with a bit of sweetness, so you won't need sugar to spruce this up. Adding vodka and espresso is just a kicker for getting whatever else you have planned for the night started on the right foot. Try the drink hot during winter months.

---

※

**GLASSWARE:** Coffee glass

**GARNISH:** Coffee beans, salt

---

- 1 ½ oz. vodka
- 1 oz. espresso
- 1 1/5 oz. Cordial Caffè Lucano Anniversario

**1.** Add all the ingredients to a mixing glass filled with ice and gently stir.

**2.** Strain the cocktail into a coffee glass.

**3.** Garnish with a few coffee beans and a pinch of salt.

## HOT VERSION

**1.** Brew espresso and pour it into a coffee glass.

**2.** Add the vodka, espresso, and Lucano and stir.

**3.** Garnish with a few coffee beans and a pinch of salt.

# TRIPLE PROPHECY

VECCHIA ROMAGNA
VIA ENRICO FERMI, 4, 40069 ZOLA PREDOSA
BOLOGNA, ITALY

Vecchia Romagna (see page 179) is a nuanced and complex brandy with notes of vanilla and spicy dashes of cinnamon. When combined with vanilla syrup, lime juice, and mint, the cocktail morphs into a smooth, refreshing drink that could become your go-to Mint Julep replacement (muddle the mint if you want more of that flavor to pop in this one). This cocktail is an ideal digestif, as mint and brandy are both classic post-dinner staples.

**GLASSWARE:** Old-fashioned glass

**GARNISH:** Aria essence or citrus twist

- 2 oz. Vecchia Romagna Tre Botti
- 1 oz. lime juice
- ½ oz. vanilla syrup
- 10 mint leaves

1. Fill an old-fashioned glass with one large ice cube.

2. Pour all the ingredients into a cocktail shaker with ice and shake vigorously.

3. Double -strain the cocktail into the old-fashioned glass.

4. Garnish with Aria essence or a citrus twist.

# CAKE SHOT

FRANGELICO
PIEDMONT, ITALY

The name of this drink is not a mistake. This shot kind of tastes like cake. Frangelico is a hazelnut liqueur, so the cake you're tasting might make you think of Nutella while the lemon wedge and citrus vodka help things go down smoothly. Careful with this one—it's so tasty, you might have to cut yourself and your friends off . . .

**GLASSWARE:** Shot glass

- 1 lemon wedge
- Sugar, as needed
- 1 oz. Frangelico
- 1 oz. SKYY Citrus Vodka

1. Run the wedge of lemon around the edge of a shot glass.

2. Dip the edge of the glass and lemon in sugar.

3. Combine the Frangelico and vodka in the shot glass.

4. Take the shot and chase it with the sugar-coated lemon wedge.

# FRANGELI-COCOA

FRANGELICO
PIEDMONT, ITALY

If your cold winter needs a hot jolt, Frangelico comes to the rescue with its version of a hot chocolate. Depending on your preference, this hot chocolate can be made with coffee, water, or milk, and is heightened with the hazelnut creaminess of Frangelico. It's either the perfect drink before going to bed (with milk or water) or a way to stay up for a few extra hours after a long meal (with coffee).

---

✳

**GLASSWARE:** Coffee mug

**GARNISH:** Whipped cream, freshly grated nutmeg

---

- 2 tablespoons hot cocoa mix
- 1 ½ oz. Frangelico
- 8 oz. hot coffee, water, or milk

1. Add the hot cocoa mix and Frangelico to a coffee mug.

2. Pour the hot coffee (or milk or water) over the mix and stir thoroughly.

3. Garnish with whipped cream and then grate fresh nutmeg over the whipped cream.

# CAFFE CORRETTO

CYNAR
PADUA, ITALY

Cynar is an Italian liqueur (see page 213) made with artichokes that has a particular bitter and herbaceous quality. Combining it with espresso will not only give you an after-dinner jolt, the flavors will meld nicely into a bittersweet mix. If your palate is bitter-shy, you can add a dash of sugar to cut this down a little.

---

✳

**GLASSWARE:** Espresso cup or coffee mug

---

• **2 oz. Cynar**

• **2 oz. espresso**

**1.** Combine the Cynar and espresso and stir. Serve warm or cold.

# VELVET WHITE ESPRESSO MARTINI

DISARONNO
SARONNO, ITALY

The dessert drink of your dreams (or maybe not since the espresso will probably keep you up), the Velvet White Espresso Martini makes good use of the incredibly smooth Disaronno Velvet that has delicate hints of almonds, chocolate, and vanilla. Combining it with vodka and the Tia Maria Liqueur gives you a boozy wake-up call if you plan on extending a dinner into a dinner party.

---

※

**GLASSWARE:** Nick & Nora glass, chilled

**GARNISH:** Chocolate flakes, 3 coffee beans

---

- 1 ½ oz. Disaronno Velvet
- ½ oz. vodka
- ½ oz. Tia Maria Cold Brew Coffee Liqueur

1. Fill a shaker with the Disaronno, vodka, Tia Maria, and ice and shake.

2. Strain the mixture into a chilled Nick & Nora.

3. Garnish with chocolate flakes and/or coffee beans.

# CAFFE SHAKERATO

AVERNA
CALTANISSETTA, SICILY

Created by Linden Pride at the venerable Dante in NYC (see page 100), the Caffe Shakerato is like an iced coffee on steroids. The combination of amaro, coffee liqueur, Appleton Reserve Rum, and fresh espresso can either be your secret morning drink to get you through the doldrums of work or the best after-dinner wake-up call to get the rest of the night started. Drink wisely, no matter what time you partake.

**GLASSWARE:** Latte glass
**GARNISH:** Orange wedge

- 1 ½ oz. fresh espresso, cooled
- 1 oz. Amaro Averna
- ½ oz. coffee liqueur
- ½ oz. agave
- ¼ oz. Appleton Estate 8 Year Old Reserve Rum
- 2 dashes Regans' Orange Bitters

1. Fill a latte glass with pebbled or crushed ice.
2. Add all the ingredients to a cocktail shaker and shake vigorously.
3. Pour the cocktail into the latte glass.
4. Garnish with an orange wedge.

# SICILIAN ESPRESSO MARTINI

AVERNA
CALTANISSETTA, SICILY

Another Averna drink created by the great Linden Pride at the historic Italian cocktail bar Dante in NYC (see page 100), the Sicilian Espresso Martini is a standout variation from the ever-popular Espresso Martini. The twist here is replacing vodka with tequila and adding the amaro (which is from Sicily). The Espolón Blanco is so smooth, you probably won't even notice the difference.

✳

**GLASSWARE:** Large coupe glass, chilled
**GARNISH:** Coffee beans

- 1 ½ oz. espresso, cooled
- 1 oz. Amaro Averna
- ½ oz. Espolón Blanco Tequila
- ½ oz. orgeat
- ¼ oz. dark crème de cacao
- 3 dashes chocolate bitters

1. Add all the ingredients to a cocktail shaker with ice and shake vigorously.

2. Strain the cocktail into a chilled coupe glass.

3. Garnish with coffee beans.

# CONTEMPORARY ITALIAN COCKTAILS:

# THE NEW WAVE OF ITALIAN COCKTAILS IN ITALY AND ABROAD

| | |
|---|---|
| GARR-IB-AWL-DEE | PANE BURRO |
| PENICILLIN COLLINS | A RABBI ONCE TOLD ME |
| SUNBURST | BIKES! |
| CALMA | NEGRON-DOG |
| ONNISCENZA | SNOW FALL MARTINI |
| SCENT | THE DESERT PUNCH |
| FRENCH | SOUR CHERRY SPRITZ |
| FOLLIA ARTISTICA | FROZEN NEGRONI |
| API DEL GIAMBOLOGNA | IL FUTURISTA |
| GIUSTI IN MANHATTAN | IL PROFESSORE |
| NEGRONI GIUSTI | SBAGLIATO ROSSO |
| PRETTY, DIRTY | CAFFE MODENA |
| COFFEY WITH MILK | IMAGINARY FRIEND |

As I outlined in the beginning of this book, there was a real inflection point in Italy around 2010. It was then that the Jerry Thomas Project (see page 32) helped usher in a new wave of cocktailing that focused on true classics, fresh ingredients, and a rigor that made bartending a true profession in the eyes of the drinking public.

Since that time, Italian bartenders who had been training and working in New York and London and other major cocktail cities began to come home to open their own bars and kick off an Italian cocktail revolution where bartenders felt free to experiment, use new technology, and push the envelope of whatever a cocktail could be.

These pioneers and their extraordinary libations are laced through this book, but in this section, they are front and center. You'll meet virtuosos like Patrick Pistolesi of Drink Kong in Rome (see page 330), Dario Comini of Nottingham Forest in Milan (see page 346), Matteo di Ienno of Locale in Florence (see page 352), and many others. You'll see recipes that call for sous vide cooking techniques, rotovapping liqueurs to remove solvents, and infusions to create new flavors and aromas.

Some of these recipes are hard and take a lot of time to make. But hopefully you'll enjoy experimenting as these cocktail alchemists are on the cutting edge of making cocktails at the very highest of levels.

# DRINK KONG WITH PATRICK PISTOLESI

## PIAZZA DI S. MARTINO AI MONTI, 8, 00154 ROMA RM, ITALY

In a world of copycats, there are only so many original thinkers, cre-ators, doers who continue to innovate, become trendsetters, change the game, and be different. Patrick Pistolesi is one of those people. As the owner and bartender of the surreal, *Blade Runner*–esque bar Drink Kong in Rome, Pistolesi wants to give customers a unique environment while exciting their tastebuds with very original cocktails.

Sure, you can get a Negroni here, and it may be the best one you ever had, but the point of Drink Kong is to go with your gut, embrace the visual elements in front of you, and let your instincts guide your drink choice. Of course, Pistolesi will be there to lead you on this drink-ing journey, but the whole point of coming to a place like this is to try something new and exciting.

As the bar motto says: Drink Kong. Think Kong. Be Kong.

### Can you tell me how you got into bartending?

I'm 44 now, and I'm half Italian half Irish which means I drink like I'm Irish and eat like an Italian. Pubs/bars have always been my life. I've been fascinated with them since I was a kid. I was blown away by going to pubs in Ireland and seeing what happens between generations talking to each other. To me it was very unusual and odd coming from Italy. But being in a pub and talking to a 60-year-old man and talking about what's going on in the town really shocked me. It was like wow, this is super, this is where the shit happens, where people get to talk.

From then on, I just started to imagine what it used to be like, you know with Hemingway's style and bars, I just got caught up in the ro-mantic part because everything we knew at the time came from books or stories and mostly movies. After high school, I got caught up in the-ater and acting, I wanted to be an actor, but I wasn't so good at cinema acting. But in theater no problem, it's still the love of my life. I still miss the rush of popping on stage. For me now, being behind the bar is the show, it's showtime. It's six o'clock in the afternoon, the audience comes in and you start the show because it's one of those jobs from seven to seven where you have to wear a smile, be nice, and stay in character, be the bartender.

### Are you in Rome at this point?

Yeah, this is all Rome. But I spent my summers in Ireland. Ireland to me meant freedom. That meant free time, free pubs, free everything. Those brief but very intense summers moved me so much. My first drink was a Piña Colada and I still remember it was made with Malibu, pineapple juice, and a dash of coconut syrup. Real shit you know, but it worked, and the guy liked it, and I liked it. When you start bartending, you get sort of a member card, like a silent member card that you're part of a guild and you're part of something, you get to other bars and people start recognizing you. I got caught up with it and one job led to another and then I was running my bar after two years, a small bar in the city center but it was packed with Americans at the time.

After that I was so caught up because the night to me was the best part of living. During the night, you get artists, weirdos, philosophers, writers, weirdly sexually oriented people, there's always great conversations running at night and every night could be a surprise where you never know what hops through that door, and that's what I like. It's where the survivors live, it's where the marginal get sheltered. That's what I like.

At the time, there was f@*king nothing in Italy, not even a cocktail book, nothing. So, my mentors were the guests. I would get the odd guy that would come back from New York and said that he would have had a Martini in this or that place, and I would beg him to teach me. My mentors were these travelers, and I was so happy to learn from them.

But once that was done, I left and started traveling. I did a little bit of England, a little bit of Ireland. I did New York. But it wasn't what I was expecting because I felt very much alone.

I came back to Italy, and I was 28 and I really didn't know at that point in my life what I wanted to do. I didn't have the money to open a bar, but still I was working shitty bars. And nobody was making real cocktails. We were still discotheque style, and it was very frustrating for me. Also, we couldn't find good bottles of stuff that I actually used abroad, and I couldn't bring my knowledge to the bars.

At one point, I got approached by the guys at the Jerry Thomas Project (see page 32). And at the time, it was called Project because it was just a fucking hole in the wall with a small bar and two bottles of bourbon. And I was like, what are we doing here, and he says, "We have to build a community. We have to show that Italians are good at what we do." And we started from scratch. We started from the *Savoy Cocktail Book*, from the *Joy of Mixology* by Gary Regan. We were sort of a club. We closed the bars at three o'clock in the morning, waited for the guys to finish their shifts, and then stay with them until seven in the morning trying drinks and discussing them.

That was the Big Bang for us. That was when the cocktail revolution started. And I was part of that.

I opened my bar four years ago and I was really influenced by Japan. I was always in love with Japan since I was a kid. You realize I'm an only child born in 1978. My father put a TV in front of me and said watch. And at the time Silvio Berlusconi was the boss of all TVs and he bought a full stock of Japanese anime that weren't good anymore in Japan, but they were huge here in Italy. Those made a real impression on me, and all the beautiful movies like *Blade Runner* and *Star Wars*. The beginning of *Blade Runner*, it says Los Angeles 2029, and they speak Japanese while

they're drinking blue drinks, and I thought what a f@*king amazing future that would be. Instead, we have the internet which could have given us omniscience but instead made us all stupid. I don't know why. It's very different than I imagined, but I wanted to put some of that imagination four years ago into my bar at Drink Kong. The whole Drink Kong project is whatever was in my head, completely poured out. The name Drink Kong comes from my best friend. So, one day, he was just sitting at the bar having drinks for free getting wasted and said, "Hey, you know you look like a f@*king ape. Like a big gorilla, you drink Kong!" And we laughed so much that the name stuck with me. So, when we opened the bar, my partner said, why don't we call it Drink Kong. So, we said f@*k it.

### Okay, can you tell me more about Drink Kong?

The whole Drink Kong project came up at the time when I wanted to be myself the most. I'll just take whatever is in my soul and see what happens. Drink Kong is like a set from *Blade Runner* or *Star Wars*, 1980s post-apocalyptic bar where you want to go and have a drink. That's why we're very classic in a way because that comes from my old school way of thinking. If you want an Old Fashioned or a Manhattan, hopefully it will be one of the best in town, because we have a huge selection, and I'm a big collector of bottles. Most bars now tend to have those minimalistic back bars with six bottles, and I tend to have about 70 Irish whiskeys, all the Japanese whiskeys ever produced. Something that we do with our menu, our menu is very visual, it's like a Rorschach test with very little information before every drink. There's big visual content with very little information that stimulates what is in the back of your brain, hopefully. And so if you get inspired by that, most of the time, you're right. Most of the time it's the thing you'll want. This is what we do and we kind of push the boundaries and be as seasonal as possible and try to break down the ingredients to make the best of the drink. A drink might be called apples or might be called blueberry or might be called snow or might be called summer. They're just bigger ideas that give you an emotion and gives some storytelling to our guests. Not a lot of garnishes, but a boost of taste and nothing too serious.

# GARR-IB-AWL-DEE

DRINK KONG
PIAZZA DI S. MARTINO AI MONTI, 8, 00154 ROMA RM,
ITALY

I'm not going to sugarcoat this—making this drink is for professionals. First, you need an electronic rotary evaporator to distill the Campari. Then, you need the ability to sous vide the orange cordial (get vacuum sealed bags for this). Now, this might sound like too much work. And it probably is. But if you want the best Garibaldi (see page 61) of your life (at home), instead of the traditional mix of orange juice and Campari, go buy some science equipment and try out Patrick Pistolesi's recipe below.

**GLASSWARE:** Tumbler glass

- **2 oz. Redistilled Campari Solution (see recipe)**
- **2 oz. Orange Cordial (see recipe)**
- **1 barspoon leftover bitters from Redistilled Campari Solution (or grapefruit bitters)**

**1.** Pour all the ingredients into a tumbler with an ice chunk and stir.

**2.** See? Easy . . .

# REDISTILLED CAMPARI SOLUTION

Use an electronic rotary evaporator to distill 17 oz. white Campari. After distilling, keep the leftover bitters for the rest of the recipe.

## ORANGE CORDIAL

Combine 6 ¾ oz. orange cordial, 3 ⅓ oz. orange curaçao, and 3 ⅓ oz. water in a vacuum-sealed sous vide bag. Heat a sous vide water bath to 135°F and cook for 2 to 3 hours. Let the bag cool and strain the ingredients using a fine mesh strainer.

# PENICILLIN COLLINS

DRINK KONG
PIAZZA DI S. MARTINO AI MONTI, 8, 00154 ROMA RM,
ITALY

**D**rink Kong is one of the most interesting bars in Rome, and bartender/owner Patrick Pistolesi is one of the most interesting bartenders. Pistolesi likes to make his own cordials, and for this version of a Penicillin, he takes his time. You'll find a great mix of smoke from the scotch, sweetness from the honey syrup, citrus from the cordial, and some fizz from the ginger beer. It's a stupendous cocktail that's well worth the wait.

---

✳

**GLASSWARE: Collins glass**

---

- 1 ½ oz. blended scotch
- 4/5 oz. Kong Cordial (see recipe)
- ½ oz. honey syrup
- Ginger beer, to top

1. Place a large ice chunk in a collins glass.

2. Combine all the ingredients, except the ginger beer, in a mixing glass with ice and stir.

3. Strain the cocktail into the collins glass and top with ginger beer.

# KONG CORDIAL

Combine 35 oz. discarded rinds from juiced limes, lemons, oranges, and grapefruit, 35 oz. sugar, and 35 oz. water in a pot and leave covered for 24 hours. Heat the mixture over medium-high, stirring until the sugar is dissolved. Reduce the heat to low and simmer for 20 minutes, stirring occasionally. Cool the mixture to room temperature and strain it through a fine mesh strainer. Add 40 grams citric acid and 20 grams malic acid. Store the cordial in a clean jar and refrigerate it when not using.

ニュー ヒューマンズ

# SUNBURST

DRINK KONG
PIAZZA DI S. MARTINO AI MONTI, 8, 00154 ROMA RM,
ITALY

Fortunately, not all of master bartender Patrick Pistolesi's drinks require a science degree. His Sunburst is simpler, and as the name suggests, is perfect for taking down before the night gets started. Here, you get a sweet and refreshing mix with a little smoke from the bourbon and a tart and fizzy finish with the grapefruit soda. The orgeat gives the cocktail hints of nuttiness, which is maybe a double entendre for Pistolesi's cocktail milieu, but the results speak for themselves.

**GLASSWARE: Collins glass**

- 1 oz. bourbon
- ⅔ oz. orgeat syrup
- ⅔ oz. honey syrup
- ⅔ oz. lime juice
- Grapefruit soda, to top

1. Add a large ice chunk to a collins glass.

2. Combine all the ingredients, except the grapefruit soda, in a mixing glass with ice and stir.

3. Strain the mixture into the collins glass.

4. Top with grapefruit soda.

# OSCAR QUAGLIARINI

Oscar Quagliarini is one of the more interesting bartenders working in Italy today. His resume speaks for itself, as he's studied under master tenders, historians, and mixologists like Stanislav Vadrna, Jeff Berry, Fernando Castellon, and others. He's worked and helped open countless bars in Italy, France, West Africa, Israel, and Mexico. Quagliarini has given seminars on bartending in Russia, Belgium, Berlin, and more. As a bartender, he's collaborated with everyone from Ardbeg and Lillet to Suntory and Beluga Vodka.

He works with flowers, spices, and perfumes by hand, producing the essences that he uses in the composition of his recipes. And he's a sought-after nose for a bevy of perfume brands because of his deep study into aromatic ingredients.

Today, the Roman-born Quagliarini splits his time between bars in Paris and Milan, and at home in the region of Marche in Italy where he works on the creation of prototypes of perfumes, liqueurs, vermouths, and distillates.

### Can you tell me how you started bartending?

I worked in Milano for eleven or twelve years for different cocktail bars and following different openings. In Italy, I was being recognized as one of the first people to use spices in cocktails and in preparing homemade ingredients. So, I got a call to go to Benin in West Africa, where I went for three months to help open this cocktail bar. And while I was there, I studied the traditional drinks of West Africa, and I started to study with the spices available over there.

After that, I got a call to come to Paris to open a cocktail bar and pizzeria called Grazie. And I stayed in Paris for three years. Then we opened Gocce in Paris that was an Italian cocktail bar with a little restaurant. And after, I helped with the opening of the Herbarium that is at the Hôtel National des Arts et Metiers, in which I still am working now, five days a month.

### How do you think about bartending today?

What I've been doing for many years now is focusing on simplicity. I try to make cocktails with a maximum of two or three ingredients. I don't use garnish, or I only use it when it makes sense. A little zest or a little rose button, I like to use the ice chunk, but all in a simple way. I am on the opposite side of these guys who use a ton of ingredients and lots of garnish. My strength is in the balancing of ingredients where you can taste everything and it's clear. And then I always create a concept behind a cocktail menu. Right now, I'm making a menu based on the tree of life in Milano, and the menu before that was inspired by the numerology of the Kabbalah. And another one, I created a cocktail menu that was inspired by the study of phrenology; with the color and the taste and the aroma I solicited a part of your brain.

# CALMA

OSCAR QUAGLIARINI

You can expect any drink that comes from the mind (and nose) of Oscar Quagliarini to have a strong and unique aroma, and his Calma is no exception. The ruby-red cocktail has a remarkable balance of spice from the pink pepper–infused gin, sweetness from the vermouth, and a complement of bitter with floral aromas from the rose bitters. It's elegant, light, and perfect for sipping alongside rich portions of foie gras or other fatty foods.

* * *

**GLASSWARE:** Old-fashioned glass

**GARNISH:** Bouton de rose

- 1 oz. gin infused with pink pepper
- 1 oz. Q Vermouth Bianco
- 1 oz. house-made rose bitters

1. Build the drink in an old-fashioned glass over an ice chunk.

2. Garnish with a bouton de rose.

# ONNISCENZA

OSCAR QUAGLIARINI

Oscar Quagliarini is famous for his original cocktails, both for how they look and for the aroma they give off. There's a reason he's a highly sought-after nose in the perfume world. This particular cocktail is simple to make and uses just three ingredients: absinthe, cucumber syrup water, and bergamot bitter. The flavor profile will be a bit herbaceous with some anise from the absinthe, refreshing sweetness from the cucumber water, and a hint of citrus bitterness from the bergamot. It's a fascinating cocktail, created by an equally fascinating mixologist. Have fun with this one at home.

**GLASSWARE:** Highball glass

**GARNISH:** Thin cucumber wheel, fine strips of lemon zest

- ½ oz. absinthe
- 4 oz. clarified cucumber syrup water
- Few drops of homemade bergamot bitter

1. Build the drink in a highball glass over an ice chunk.

2. Add the absinthe.

3. Add the clarified cucumber syrup water.

4. Add drops of the bergamot bitter until you create a thin layer of green on top.

5. Garnish with a thin cucumber wheel and fine strips of lemon zest.

# NOTTINGHAM FOREST

## VIALE PIAVE, 1, 20129 MILANO MI, ITALY

There's nothing quite like Nottingham Forest in Milan and there is no one quite like owner Dario Comini. The bar itself opened in 1970, but Comini has managed/owned it since 1976. When you walk inside the low-lit space, your eyes dart around the room as sensory overload takes over from the vast array of collectibles hanging from the walls and ceiling, brought back from Comini's travels around the world.

Consistently ranked in the World's 50 Best Bars, Nottingham has a reputation for pushing the envelope of where cocktailing can go. Comini is a pioneer of techniques, borrowing and sharing with the world of molecular gastronomy to create a new class of wild and inventive cocktails.

Here's a bit more from the impresario himself. Then, try to make some of his elaborate cocktails on the next few pages.

### Tell me about the bar.

The Nottingham was opened in 1970. The walls of the room are covered with a rough and very hard wood from the island of Antigua. This type of wood used by the "Caribis," the ancient natives of the Caribbean, to build canoes, is a waterproof and very hard wood that allows the thermal insulation of the room by keeping the temperature around 20°C in all seasons, without heating. The decor is made up of hundreds of objects collected from my travels around the world (sharks, crocodiles, cobras, ritual masks, oriental jewels, etc.). Nottingham has been voted one of the fifty best bars in the world for over a decade and has reached fifteenth place in the world so far the highest ranked Italian bar since the rankings exist.

### What kind of cocktails are you making?

For many years, the type of mixing proposed has been avant-garde. There are many creations that have become a world trend for us: alcoholic spherification, smoke bubbles, velvets, etc. They were all born here. Pioneers in molecular blending, my books have been the foundation for the study of the profession for decades. Despite the type of modern mix, the restaurant offers a relaxed and comfortable atmosphere, with leather sofas and seats suitable for a few couples and not for large companies, so as not to affect the romantic atmosphere.

### Where do you see cocktailing going in the future?

I see the future of the cocktail increasingly linked to technological discovery, the possibility of printing on liquids, machines that dehydrate liqueurs, etc. Technological research will allow new developments in our field, and we must be ready to implement it.

# SCENT

**D**ario Comini is the mad scientist behind the clever creations inside the ethereal Nottingham Forest in Milan. He's considered the godfather of Italy's molecular mixology movement, and his cocktails are a feast for all of your senses. The combination of limoncello, vermouth, and gin in Scent brings together bitter, tart, and sweet flavors—but the unexpected comes with the spray of perfume that has notes of vanilla and citrus to help enhance the entire drinking experience.

**GLASSWARE:** Coupe glass (Mamo)

**GARNISH:** The One by Dolce & Gabbana

- 1 oz. Limoncello Lucano
- 1 oz. gin
- 1 oz. Lucano Vermouth del Cavaliere

**1.** Fill a coupe glass with ice.

**2.** Add all the ingredients and stir.

**3.** Spray The One by Dolce & Gabbana on the outside of the glass.

# FRENCH

Nothing can quite prepare you for the otherworldliness of the cocktail program inside Nottingham Forest in Milan. The team uses a plethora of scientific methods to infuse, confuse, and create drinks that may sound familiar but are something else entirely. Lucky for us, they share a simpler cocktail here. The French is a tricolor drink meant to mirror the French flag (blue, white, red) and combines the bittersweetness of Amaro Lucano with the effervescence of sparkling wine, along with a hint of seaweed from the spirulina-laced vodka. Visually stunning and fun to drink, this cocktail will be a hit at any party—especially for any Francophiles.

**GLASSWARE:** Gin highball glass

**GARNISH:** Orange essence

- 5 to 6 oz. brut sparkling wine
- ⅔ oz. Amaro Lucano
- ⅔ oz. vodka, colored blue with spirulina

1. Pour the sparkling wine into a highball glass.

2. Add the amaro and allow it to collect at the bottom.

3. Top off the drink with the vodka, one spoon at a time to preserve the color layers.

4. Spray the glass with orange essence.

# LOCALE

Easily the most interesting bar/restaurant in Florence, Locale is set off on a narrow, nondescript side street, but waiting inside is an apothecary of cocktail-making carved out of an ancient palace. The man behind the bevy of fascinating cocktails that change with the seasons is Matteo di Ienno. Here's a one-on-one with Matteo and some fascinating recipes that follow.

### How did you get into bartending?

I started bartending very early when I was only 16 in my family bar. I started my career at five-star hotels when I was about 19. But Florence was a bit small for me, so I left for London, where I worked for one year at the Brown's Hotel in Mayfair. After a year I came back to Florence for the opening of the Four Seasons Firenze in 2008 and I spent three years of my life bartending there. After that I left for New York and spent one year working in a small trattoria. I had some Visa issues, so I moved back to London, where I worked at a private membership only club, and I think it was the top of the hospitality world I ever reached. It was called 5 Hertford Street. Only very important people were coming there. Also, the BAFTA Awards were hosted there and many events with Leonardo DiCaprio and George Clooney, whomever you can think about. After a year of that I decided to move to another bar because London is full of great bars, and I was 26 at the time. I worked at The Edition Hotel opening and it was the third startup of my career. And that is where I started to work with homemade stuff, and more complicated cocktails as it was the trend at the time. After almost three years there, I was offered the position as bar manager at Locale.

### How would you describe your bartending philosophy today?

I have to say, I'm getting old enough to have seen a lot of change in the bar industry. When we opened Locale in 2015, it was all about showing off the garnishes and cooking skills behind them. The trend

today is more minimal, a focus on flavors. We've reached a time where people don't want to wait for a cocktail. I would say our first cocktail list in 2018 was all focused on storytelling in Florence. We were talking about little stories of Florence that were expressed in cocktails that were related to the city, so maybe someone would then go to a statue that was written on the menu. We wanted to make them curious about the city by drinking our drinks. But it was a lot to read. So, after a year we launched our second cocktail list, which was inspired by the Italian gestures, which is really cool because we basically translated words with our hands and the guests loved it because they would order a drink with just a gesture. You know we're quite famous in Italy because we talk with our hands. Then our last cocktail list is more focused on flavors and trying to use all the local fresh ingredients, and stuff that is seasonal in Italy. I came up with the menu so we could change it with the seasons.

# FOLLIA ARTISTICA

LOCALE

VIA DELLE SEGGIOLE, I2R, 50I22 FIRENZE FI, ITALY

The translation of *Follia Artistica* is "Artistic Madness," and when looking at the ingredients of this impressive cocktail by Matteo di Ienno of Locale in Florence, it's easy to see why. The way Ienno puts it, "It is known that all artists have moments of madness. Often in the Renaissance opium was used as a creative means, therefore we were inspired by the madness of artists using vapors of CBD weed." This particular cocktail will have a mix of flavors: smooth, caramel-esque notes from the tequila, tartness from the bergamot, fruity tang from the red fruit shrub, and some smoky herbal hits from the weed. Visually, the drink is a showstopper; taste-wise, it's a beautiful system shocker, and the effect . . . well, that all depends on which weed you're using and how much you consume—warning you here . . .

**GLASSWARE:** Ball flask

- 1 ⅓ oz. Don Julio 1942
- ⅔ oz. bergamot liqueur
- ⅔ oz. seasonal clarified citrus
- ⅓ oz. red fruit shrub
- 1 gram per vape of vaporized legal marijuana

**1.** Add all the ingredients, except the marijuana, to a mixing glass with ice and stir.

**2.** Strain the mixture into a ball flask.

3. Surround the ball flask with a clear plastic bag.

4. Insert large straw through the flask opening.

5. Blow one vape of vaporized legal marijuana into the plastic bag and seal the bag with the straw sticking out.

# API DEL GIAMBOLOGNA

LOCALE
VIA DELLE SEGGIOLE, 12R, 50122 FIRENZE FI, ITALY

The bartending team at Locale are known for whimsical and multi-layered cocktails with fascinating origin stories. This one is no exception. As bartender Matteo di Ienno explains, "Arriving in Piazza Santissima Annunziata, one finds oneself in front of the monument of Ferdinando I de' Medici, a work created by Giambologna and Pietro Tacca. The monument has a double meaning, as another was created behind the first statue: a queen bee and a swarm of worker bees arranged all around in such a way as to confuse anyone who tries to count them. It is said that when children insistently asked their parents for something, their parents promised them that they would grant their wishes as long as they were able to count the bees on Ferdinando I's sign, obviously never successfully." This cocktail is an ode to the sculpture and aptly named "Bees by Giambologna." With a combination of rum, turmeric milk, pimento, and orange liqueurs, this drink will be sweet and spicy and remind you of a swarm of honeybees flying around the stunning statues of Florence.

**GLASSWARE: Playful mug**

**GARNISH: Grilled pineapple, raspberries, nettle**

- 1 ⅔ oz. Matusalem Gran Reserva 15-Year Rum
- 1 ⅓ oz. tepache
- ½ oz. honey
- ⅓ oz. golden (turmeric) milk
- ⅓ oz. pimento dram
- 1/6 oz. orange liqueur

1. Add all the ingredients to a cocktail shaker with ice and shake.

2. Strain the cocktail into a mug.

3. Garnish with grilled pineapple, raspberry, and nettle.

# GIUSTI

## PIAZZA GRANDE 38/39, 41121 MODENA MO, ITALY

The Giusti family has been producing balsamic vinegar in Modena since 1605 and is the oldest balsamic producer still in business today. The company continues to be run by the same family and is well known for selling the highest-quality balsamic vinegar in the world.

One of the newest trends in cocktails is to take balsamic vinegar and incorporate it into drinks. On the surface, this might sound strange, but if you've ever tried balsamic on chocolate, or vanilla ice cream, or Parmigiano cheese, you'll know how that vinegar enhances flavors in very exciting ways.

The bartending community has picked up on this idea and the cocktail world is only getting better for it. In the following pages, you'll find some exquisite Giusti cocktail recipes, like a Giusti Manhattan (see page 362) and a Giusti Negroni (see page 365), and more.

I talked to the CEO of Giusti, Claudio Stefani, to get into the history of the company and how they're using balsamic to change cocktail making around the globe.

### Can we start with some Giusti history and then how we got to using balsamic in cocktails?

The story of Giusti is long and amazing. We tell it at the museum here that we built five years ago. For example, our iconic label was designed more than 100 years ago. My family was also a supplier of the

king of Italy for balsamic vinegar, so there are many things to be told to underline how old of a company we are. We are the oldest producer of balsamic vinegar that exists today. My work has been to take the product and bring it back to its origin, bring back the quality and to study the story as much as I could.

But when it comes to innovation, balsamic vinegar doesn't really allow a lot of innovation on the product itself. Technology may help, but when it's using great raw materials, working according to the tradition, you can improve it only so much. Balsamic is a product that is protected like Chianti in wine. You don't do a lot of innovation on the wine. So, what we decided was to innovate the company and under us we have tried to be everywhere, from advertising to research. If you get one of our good balsamic vinegars and try it on a dessert like ice cream, you'll realize that it's very good, because you have to imagine that it's not liquid and acidic, but it's sour, and nice and thick. And above all, the thickness changes the sourness and makes it much more appealing to your palate. So, we wanted to create a world and renew balsamic vinegar to create something a bit more fancy and younger. We actually tried to see how it could have been in cocktails. Why, because in cocktails they use shrubs. And shrubs come from the tradition of keeping alive fruit juice thanks to alcohol or vinegar. Because the juice wouldn't last, and it was easier to add something that makes it last like vinegar. So, we found a special balance with the cocktails and that brought us to the world of vermouth and to the Negroni and the Milano-Torino. But not all of them work because vinegar brings two things. One is acidity. And the other one is the flavor—balsamic is full of balsamic flavor and aroma. And we saw here and there that some barmen around the world were already using it. And so, we found that they were interested and were making cocktails that were fantastically amazing. After that, we created a vermouth as well with these similarities and philosophies because vermouth is a wine product and it felt similar to our world of making balsamic.

# GIUSTI IN MANHATTAN

GIUSTI
PIAZZA GRANDE 38/39, 41121 MODENA MO, ITALY

There's no more classic of a cocktail than a Manhattan. Rye, vermouth, bitters—simple and great. And since its creation in the 1870s, there have been subtle changes, but nothing quite like this. Giusti, the oldest balsamic vinegar company in the world, wanted to dress the Manhattan up a bit by using their own sweet vermouth and adding their vintage balsamic. It takes the otherwise smooth and sophisticated version of the Manhattan and adds a richness with a bit of tang that'll make you rethink ordering it any differently again.

**GLASSWARE:** Coupe glass, chilled

**GARNISH:** Lemon twist

- 1 oz. rye whiskey
- 1 oz. Vermouth Giusti
- 2 dashes Angostura bitters
- 2 barspoons Giusti Balsamic Vinegar

1. Add all the ingredients to a mixing glass filled with ice and stir until well chilled.

2. Strain the cocktail into a chilled coupe.

3. Garnish with a lemon twist.

# NEGRONI GIUSTI

GIUSTI

PIAZZA GRANDE 38/39, 41121 MODENA MO, ITALY

Giusti is the oldest balsamic vinegar maker in the world, so they know a thing or two about their products and how to pair them. For this Negroni recipe, Giusti simply adds their sweet, sticky, complex vinegar to a classic and it elevates the Negroni in unforeseen ways. It's richer, a little sweeter, and even tangier. The flavors do a little dance and scramble your brain. It's stellar.

---

✳

**GLASSWARE:** Old-fashioned glass

**GARNISH:** Orange peel

---

- 1 oz. Vermouth Giusti
- 1 oz. Campari
- 1 oz. gin
- 2 barspoons Giusti Balsamic Vinegar, plus 1 barspoon for garnish

1. Fill an old-fashioned glass with ice.

2. Add the vermouth, Campari, gin, and 2 barspoons of balsamic vinegar to a mixing glass with ice and stir until well chilled.

3. Strain the mixture into the old-fashioned glass.

4. Garnish with an orange peel and another barspoon of balsamic vinegar.

# PRETTY, DIRTY

GUCCI OSTERIA DA MASSIMO BOTTURA
347 N RODEO DR, BEVERLY HILLS, CA 90210

Gucci Osteria da Massimo Bottura is one of the finest Italian restaurants in Beverly Hills (the flagship is in Florence). The whimsical locale is Michelin-starred with a slew of have-to-see-them-to-believe-them Italian dishes. Complementing the creative food is the equally impressive cocktail menu created by bartender Christian Philippo. This first cocktail is the bar's version of a Dirty Martini with a lot of surprises that include an olive oil granita, and a blue cheese–stuffed olive. This drink requires a bit of work, but the payoff will have your guests filling their social media feeds with the end result.

**GLASSWARE:** Martini glass

**GARNISH:** Rogue River blue cheese–stuffed olive

- **2 ¼ oz. Chopin Extra Rare Young Potato Vodka**
- **3 drops saline water (see page 23)**
- **¾ oz. Dirty Sue Premium Olive Juice**
- **Olive Oil Granita (see recipe), to top**

1. Fill a cocktail shaker with ice.

2. Add the vodka, saline, and olive juice and shake vigorously.

3. Strain the mixture into a martini glass.

4. Top the drink with a large spoonful of granita.

5. Garnish with a blue cheese-filled olive.

# OLIVE OIL GRANITA

In a medium saucepan, combine 8 oz. water and 4 oz. granulated sugar and heat the mixture over medium heat, stirring until the sugar dissolves. Remove the pan from heat and add 4 oz. extra virgin olive oil and ¼ oz. sea salt and stir. Add 2 oz. lemon juice and stir. Pour the mixture into a shallow container and freeze. After 30 minutes, use a fork to scrape the mixture into ice crystals. Return the mixture to the freezer and repeat this process every 30 minutes, until the granita is frozen and has a fluffy texture.

# COFFEY WITH MILK

GUCCI OSTERIA DA MASSIMO BOTTURA
347 N RODEO DR, BEVERLY HILLS, CA 90210

One of the most interesting and beautiful drinks on the Gucci Osteria menu created by bartender Christian Philippo is the Coffey with Milk. The name doesn't really do it justice, as this cocktail blends Japanese and Italian flavors and uses Nikka Coffey Gin—where "coffey" refers to the copper pots they use at the Nikka distillery. It's a play on the Italian caffè latte, or coffee with milk, and combines fascinating flavors of bitterness from the Luxardo, fruitiness from the sake, and dryness from the vermouth. It's a killer cocktail that is a must for any burgeoning bartender to try at home.

**GLASSWARE:** Rocks glass

**GARNISH:** Lemon slice, cherry

- 1 ½ oz. Nikka Coffey Gin
- ¾ oz. Pio Cesare Bianco Vermouth
- ¾ oz. Luxardo Bitter Bianco
- ¼ oz. Sho Chiku Bai Nigori Unfiltered Sake

1. Add ice to a rocks glass.

2. Add all the ingredients, except the sake, to a shaker with ice and shake vigorously.

3. Strain the mixture into rocks glass.

4. Add the sake to create the milky effect.

# JULIAN BIONDI

## FLORENCE, ITALY

Julian Biondi is a bartender, bar consultant, teacher, journalist, and entrepreneur. He's widely known for his exceptional mixology skills that
have won him multiple bartending competitions around the world.

Today, he splits his time writing for *Bargiornale*, the most important
bar magazine in Italy, helping bars create their own spirits through his
company, Fermenthinks, and teaching chefs how to create killer cocktail
pairings at Le Cordon Bleu.

Julian has an interesting outlook on bartending culture in Italy and is
an incredible resource for where the country is headed in the world of
cocktails. Take a read and then see some of his stellar cocktail creations
on the following pages.

### Can you tell me how you got into bartending and the world of mixology?

I was born and raised in Florence, and like many of us, I started bartending during university, where I studied communication and journalism.
Once I finished school, bartending became a passion and I wanted to
combine my two passions [the other one was writing]. I started [writing]
for this Italian magazine called *Bargiornale*. It happened spontaneous-
ly—I went to Russia for the first time (my wife is Russian), and I met a lot
of interesting people in the bar community. I wrote an article about the
Moscow bar scene and sent it to them, and they liked it.

I worked in a bar about nine years ago called Rivalta. We were one
of the first ones to invest in this new trend of gin and we had like 100
types of gin, and we started to do what was already going on outside
the country, which was this new cocktail revolution. It was a great experience, but the next one for me was even more relevant—Caffè Florian
in Florence, which was a branch of the very famous Caffè Florian in
Venice, the oldest café in Italy, from 1720. We were the first ones
making ginger beer and making tonic by ourselves, carving the ice, and
so on. It was an elegant venue, and we were getting well reviewed for
doing new stuff.

This was in 2015, 2016. It was the year in which Florence Cocktail Week was born. This event is quite important to understand a bit more why Florence nowadays is one of the three most important cities for drinking in Italy. In 2016 we had thirteen cocktail bars, and this year there will be forty-five venues. I think it gave the opportunity to bartenders to show themselves to bars and to be more creative, and to get people to know a little bit more about the drinking culture in the town. Then it became a national event, and an international event. The first year, there was a competition, and I won the competition. So, this gave me a little bit of popularity in town.

And what we did one year ago with Matteo di Ienno (see page 352) and Stefano Cicalese, we created Fermenthinks, which is a distillery that helps bars create their own labels. At Le Cordon Bleu, I teach chefs how to pair with cocktails and basically how to make cocktails without being a bartender.

**What have you seen change in the Italian cocktail world in the last five years?**

Five years ago, Milan and Rome weren't the only places to drink in Italy. Florence came, but also Bologna and Naples. The cocktail culture spread in cities like Lecce and Palermo. What has happened in the last three years is that many other smaller cities became relevant in terms of having at least two or three nice watering holes. In Italy now, you can have a good drink in small cities.

Professional bartenders are not yet like professional chefs—who are superstars—but [bartending came] to be seen as a profession. When I started bartending, I wasn't sure if I wanted to say that; it was just my other job to make a living. Now, it's seen by older people as a real job. So, we invest in our training, we invest in our job, and we invest in knowing more and more and this is something which is strange to say by an Italian because Italians have always made [bartending] a profession. You find Italians everywhere in the hospitality industry and they are professional in what they do, but only because the [local] environment allowed them to become professionals. Working in hospitality in the U.S. is considered a real job and a real career. And now it's becoming like this also here, but it's still a bit slow.

# PANE BURRO

JULIAN BIONDI
FLORENCE, ITALY

Julian Biondi is the winner of multiple bartending competitions for a reason. He consistently surprises and amazes with his original concoctions, and this cocktail is a great example of it. It's based on a typical Italian breakfast crossed with a twisted, Russian version of a Negroni. It'll take a bit to make it because you'll need to fat-wash the Campari and infuse your vermouth, but the end result is worth it, and you'll only have to do the hard parts once. Enjoy your Italian breakfast cocktail any time of day (but preferably at night).

---

✳

**GLASSWARE: Rocks glass**

**GARNISH: Burnt lime wheel**

---

- 1 oz. Polugar Rye & Wheat Vodka
- 1 oz. Jammouth (see recipe)
- 1 oz. Butter Campari (see recipe)

1. Add ice to a rocks glass.

2. Add all the ingredients to the glass and stir.

3. Garnish with a burnt lime wheel.

# JAMMOUTH

Pour 1 jar of orange jam into a saucepan and heat it over low until it becomes more liquid. Add ¼ cup Carpano Antica Red Vermouth and stir until fully combined. Increase the heat to medium-low and simmer for 10 to 15 minutes, stirring occasionally. Remove the pan from heat and allow the mixture to cool. Strain the mixture through a fine mesh strainer into a jar. Seal it with an airtight lid and store it in the refrigerator.

# BUTTER CAMPARI

Melt 1 stick unsalted butter in a saucepan over low heat. Add 1 bottle of Campari to the pan and stir to combine. Increase the heat to medium-low and stir for 10 minutes. Remove the mixture from heat and let it cool. Strain it through a fine mesh strainer to remove any butter solids. Place the butter-fat-washed Campari in the refrigerator until the fat solidifies and can be skimmed off.

# A RABBI ONCE TOLD ME

JULIAN BIONDI
FLORENCE, ITALY

O ne of my favorite drinks is a French 75, but in the bar where I used to work, we were not serving Champagne by the glass, because there was a serious risk that the staff (mostly me) would drink the bottle once open," Julian Biondi says. "In that period, I was also a big fan of shrubs, and somewhere I read about this celery shrub that was used in the Jewish community of Brooklyn. It was basically celery syrup and apple cider vinegar. They would add it to sparkling wine to give it a more yellow color and an acidity similar to Champagne and they would call the beverage 'the Jewish Champagne.' I found my way to a very good twist on a French 75 thanks to this little secret coming from the Jewish culture."

---

＊

**GLASSWARE:** Coupe glass

**GARNISH:** Lemon peel

---

- 1 ⅔ oz. Sipsmith London Dry Gin
- 4/5 oz. lemon juice
- ⅓ oz. egg whites
- ⅔ oz. Raspberry Shrub (see recipe)
- Prosecco, to top

**1.** Add all the ingredients, except the prosecco, to a cocktail shaker with ice and shake vigorously.

**2.** Strain the mixture into a coupe and top with prosecco.

**3.** Garnish with a lemon peel.

# RASPBERRY SHRUB

Combine 500 grams raspberries and 800 grams sugar in a large glass and mash until the sugar is dissolved. Wait 24 hours. Add 400 grams apple cider vinegar and shake to fully combine. Strain the shrub through a fine mesh strainer and store in an airtight jar in the refrigerator for up to 1 month.

# THE LET'S GO! DISCO & COCKTAIL CLUB

## 710 E 4TH PL, LOS ANGELES, CA 90013

Probably the most fun you'll ever have drinking Italian cocktails is courtesy of The Let's Go! Disco & Cocktail Club in downtown Los Angeles. Opened at the end of 2022, the bar is meant to evoke 1970s and 1980s southern Italian vibes, but fortunately for all of us, with much better drinks.

While there's an unserious nature bandied about here, there's nothing funny about the cocktail program. Led by Lee Zaremba (one of the opening bartenders at the amaro heaven Billy Sunday cocktail bar in Chicago), the booze bottles lining the shelves behind the bar are lousy with obscure amari, rare Italian gins, and Italian liqueurs that true Italophiles will know and appreciate.

Cocktails run the gamut from a version of a Bicyclette called BIKES! (see page 380) to an exceptional rendition of a Negroni dubbed Negron-Dog (see page 382).

Zaremba's resume also includes opening almost a dozen bars for the Boka Restaurant Group in Chicago, the most important being Lazy Bird inside the Hoxton Hotel, which was named Hotel Bar of the Year in 2020. Zaremba has also published his own cocktail book and is an expert on amaro.

The Let's Go! Disco & Cocktail Club is part of a new wave of Italian bars popping up around the United States, and this spot is easily the most unpretentious and entertaining of the bunch.

# BIKES!

The Let's Go! is one of the most exciting new bars in Los Angeles, and it specializes in Italian cocktails. Bartender Lee Zaremba likes to mix things up to keep customers on their toes, and this cocktail is his version of a Bicyclette. The original Bicyclette is made with just Campari and white wine, but Zaremba adds a saffron soda that not only brings out a beautiful yellow color, but it also adds some taste complexity and some fizz that makes for a great summer cocktail.

✳

**GLASSWARE:** Collins glass

**GARNISH:** Lemon half-wheel

- 4 oz. saffron soda
- 1 oz. Campari
- 1 oz. dry white wine

1. Add ice to a collins glass.

2. Add all the ingredients to the collins glass and stir.

3. Garnish with a half-wheel of lemon.

# NEGRON-DOG

THE LET'S GO! DISCO & COCKTAIL CLUB
710 E 4TH PL, LOS ANGELES, CA 90013

Lee Zaremba, the head bartender at The Let's Go! says that this drink is "a look into the past; a soft, floral, and less bitter Negroni." That's probably a fair self-assessment, as the Meletti Amaro is smoother than most amari, and the red bitter blend doesn't have the same bitter bite that Campari brings to the table. No matter, it's a very well-balanced drink that will have you thinking hard about taking that one extra step to make a Negroni if you're a fan of a slightly sweeter version.

**GLASSWARE:** Rocks glass

**GARNISH:** Orange peel stars

- 1 ½ oz. Hayman's Old Tom Gin
- ¾ oz. Cocchi Vermouth di Torino
- ½ oz. red bitter blend (60/40 Luxardo Red Bitter and Gran Classico Bitter)
- ¼ oz. Meletti Amaro

1. Add a large ice cube to a rocks glass.

2. Add all the ingredients to a mixing glass with ice and stir for 10 to 12 seconds.

3. Strain the cocktail into the rocks glass.

4. Garnish with orange peel stars.

# MARIANTONIETTA VARAMO

In a profession that is completely dominated by men, especially in Italy, it can be hard for a woman to break through and be seen as a top-level bartender. Mariantonietta Varamo is one of those women who, through perseverance and determination, rose through the bartending ranks to achieve that level of status when she bartended at Dukes in London, one of the best bars in the world.

Check out my one-on-one with this amazing Italian mixologist, and see one of her stunning recipes that follows.

### Can you tell me about yourself and how you got into bartending?

I was born in the south of Italy in Calabria, but I grew up in Tuscany. My bartending passion started in a very funny way. It was during the summertime with my parents, and we were going to the seaside, and I was one of the kids who was going to buy gelato for a snack. My father used to have a little aperitivo like a Campari Soda or some bitter, and they give you some nuts and crisps. The people behind the bar were always super friendly and always happy and pleased to see you. I looked at them and they seemed like really cool people, so I decided that's what I wanted to do. I went to hospitality school in Italy and during the summertime, I was doing jobs at the seaside around Tuscany. I worked in some hotels and one summer one of the hotels said I need to improve my English so I can grow in my career here in Italy. And I was like, okay, I'm gonna do a couple of months in London and then I'll be back.

I came by the Dukes Hotel, where I started in 2012, and at the time, there were no positions open for bartenders. So, I started as a waiter in the restaurant. But after three months, the guy who started the same day as me, but at the bar, left, and they said to me, we have a vacancy, I don't know if you're interested but just for you to know, this is a male kind of bar. Meaning that no woman had ever worked there as a bartender. So, the customers might not be used to you and maybe some of them could be affected by it. And I was like, okay, I really, want to try. I'm very petite as a person and I'm very smiley and friendly so as soon as you see me, I don't come across as scary or whatever. I ended up working at Dukes for five or six years.

**What kinds of cocktails were you making at Dukes?**

I was coming from an Italian experience where cocktails are very much open to what the guest wants, meaning that you don't have one type of bar. But when I moved to Dukes, we were oriented in Martini cocktails and classic cocktails like Manhattans, Old Fashioneds. So, I was expanding my knowledge on the classics. And I really did refine my palate there, as well.

**Let's talk about being an Italian woman in this very male-dominated world. What do you think it's going to be like in the future?**

There is a little bit more opening for women at the moment, but still there is a lot of work to do. I mean, you will always be a woman no matter what. It's not that I want to be harsh, but in Italy, you will still be looked at as a woman, not as a person who has the ability and skills to make your business grow. So, to give an example, there are jobs being advertised where they're asking for two women bartenders to do seasonal jobs in Rimini or in the Riviera. And when I'm looking at those job offers, which, maybe they are good job offers, but why do you have to put a gender on there? And when there is a woman bartender working in a bar, it's emphasized so much, like they're making such an effort to let you know, that it doesn't feel genuine. You can get this attitude of, "I'm the one allowing you to be here, so just remember this"—on one hand praising you, but on the other wanting credit for putting you there.

**Does it make you question whether you want to be doing this?**

I'm coming from a position where I feel free to speak my mind because I know that I am a person. But if I'm going back to Italy, I'll have to really bite my tongue on many, many occasions. But in London, we are extremely politically correct, and in a way that sometimes is really like, oh my god guys, relax. But Italy is the opposite.

# SNOW FALL MARTINI

## MARIANTONIETTA VARAMO

Bartender Mariantonietta Varamo loves making beautiful cocktails and this is probably at the top of her list. The Snow Fall Martini is a really stunning take on a traditional Martini with the addition of violette liqueur to give it a floral aroma and a purple color, but also the chamomile liqueur to add citrus notes to the drink. Martini purists won't really know what to do with themselves, but give it a try—you might just be persuaded to drink them like this from now on.

**GLASSWARE: Martini glass, chilled**
**GARNISH: Lemon zest, rose and/or violette petals**

- **2 oz. Snow Queen Vodka, frozen**
- **⅔ oz. Martini Bianco Vermouth**
- **⅓ oz. chamomile liqueur**
- **1/6 oz. violette liqueur**

**1.** Pour all the ingredients into a mixing glass with ice and gently stir.

**2.** Strain the cocktail into a chilled martini glass.

**3.** Garnish with lemon zest.

**4.** Affix rose and/or violette petals around the rim of the glass.

# L'ANTIQUARIO AND ALEX FREZZA

## VIA VANNELLA GAETANI, 2, 80121 NAPOLI NA, ITALY

You always know you're in for something serious when the servers behind the bar are rocking lab coats. And the moment you poke your head through the small, nondescript wooden door on a Napoli side street, the weighty business of drinking intricate cocktails begins.

The atmosphere inside L'Antiquario is dark and brooding with all the focus on the stunning backlit bar that screams gothic church organ grinder meets apothecary. Owner and head bartender Alex Frezza is the brains behind this Naples anomaly and has helped put this frenetic and energetic metropolis on the international cocktail map.

### How did you get into cocktailing?

I was lucky enough that when I started getting interested in cocktails, it was the early 2000s and it was very lively, and it was a period where everything was changing. And I got caught up in the good part of it. I was drinking in London in 2007 when the new cool bars were opening.

### How do you think about cocktail culture broadly in Italy?

We have a drinking culture in Italy that extends very far back actually, but not in mixed drinks. Our culture is more about digestifs and cordials. And that's transformed into aperitifs. But we also have a very strong culture around wine, which connects to aperitifs in many ways. Cocktails are kind of a foreign thing here and have that kind of fascination because you drink cocktails at different times. For Italians, that's a bit strange, because we have aperitifs before we eat, wine while we eat, and then digestifs after. For cocktails, we kind of classify them in those areas.

### How does being in Naples inspire your bartending?

Our last menu was called the Napoli Capitale. "Capital" is a word that means many things: it means how much you're worth, what is important to you, what is your value, and it also has a political context. And when we opened L'Antiquario, it was born in that thread of the classic European cocktail bars. Like they are in Venice, in Vienna, in Paris, some in London, and so on. We decided to make things international. If you come to L'Antiquario, you could drink a Manhattan just like you had it in Las Vegas two days before. So, we spent the first six to seven years competing to be good at an international level in the classics.

After COVID, we kind of changed our attitude because we learned to do many things and we were satisfied by it. We started doing a bit more regarding our way of drinking in Italy or in Naples. Sometimes it's more of an expectation of tourists to drink something that's local. So, in this cocktail list, it's more about storytelling about the city of Naples, because that's what people wanted more. We make a cocktail called Volcano Daisy, with little apricots that are grown on Mt. Vesuvius. Getting your hands on those apricots is extremely difficult; we manage once or twice a year, and we make jam out of them. We're not a bar that can change our menu every two weeks or every month. We have to keep it there for at least six months because I want people to be able to come back and find the same cocktail and not have to always adapt to new things.

### Are you seeing any new cocktail trends in Naples or Italy more broadly?

I never thought I would have to have a nonalcoholic cocktail at L'Antiquario, but I'm putting one in now. I don't know how that will evolve; it might just fade away in a couple of years. But that is surely something that's happening. And it's to a point where a Gin & Tonic is an aperitif in Italy and it's considered a go-to drink for the basic drinker.

### Do you think that people are more educated about cocktails than ever before?

I always make this comparison between wine and cocktails. The average 35-year-old in Naples, or in most of the big cities in Italy, has done some sort of course on wine. That means when they order wine in the restaurants, they know what they're speaking about. It's a bit more difficult in cocktails because cocktails are much more complicated. You have to learn all sorts of different spirits, liqueurs, the way they're put together, the rules in which to put them together, and the history of the cocktails. It's so much more information, and people are slowly getting there. Take the Boulevardier: that's a cocktail that wasn't drunk in Naples ten years ago. Now it's a common cocktail for people.

# THE DESERT PUNCH

L'ANTIQUARIO AND ALEX FREZZA
VIA VANNELLA GAETANI, 2, 80121 NAPOLI NA, ITALY

This punch-style drink by Alex Frezza is inspired by the North African mint tea tradition. Gin combines well with the tea, and the orange curaçao and the fernet give it a slight bitterness. It's a long and soothing cocktail to be enjoyed with a group of people.

✳

**GLASSWARE: Small tea glasses and a Moroccan tea pot**
**GARNISH: Sprig of mint**

- 2 oz. gin
- 2 oz. gunpowder mint tea
- ¾ oz. muscovado sugar syrup
- ¼ oz. orange curaçao
- 1 oz. lime juice
- 1/6 oz. fernet

1. Mix all the ingredients in a shaker and "throw" from one tin with ice to another without ice.

2. Do this four to five times until the cocktail is cold and nice and frothy.

3. Pour the drink into a Moroccan teapot and serve in small tea glasses with a sprig of mint.

# SOUR CHERRY SPRITZ

CAPRI CLUB
4604 EAGLE ROCK BLVD, LOS ANGELES, CA 90041

Capri Club has a long and distinguished history as a restaurant and bar in the Eagle Rock neighborhood of Los Angeles. Originally named The Capri Italian Restaurant when it opened in 1963, it's since changed hands and reopened in 2022 as Capri Club by hospitality veteran Robert Fleming.

Capri Club is part of a trend happening in the United States where Italian cocktails are becoming more prevalent, and the concept of *la dolce vita* ("the good life") is becoming more *di moda*. So, flip through Capri Club's delicious creations and create a little of la dolce vita in your own house.

Be careful with this cocktail. It tastes exactly like a cherry cola, yet it has a pretty high ABV. Regardless of how drunk it can get you, it's really nice on a hot summer day before gorging yourself on pasta.

**GLASSWARE:** Wine glass

**GARNISH:** Maraschino cherry, cherry syrup

- ¾ oz. Marendry Amarena Wild Cherry Aperitivo
- ½ oz. Bordiga Maraschino
- ½ oz. vodka
- Splash of soda water
- Prosecco, to top

1. Combine the aperitivo, Bordiga, and vodka in a wine glass and then add a splash of soda.

2. Add ice to the top of the glass and then top with prosecco.

3. Garnish with a maraschino cherry and a half-barspoon of syrup from the cherries.

# FROZEN NEGRONI

CAPRI CLUB
4604 EAGLE ROCK BLVD, LOS ANGELES, CA 90041

Now this is a summer treat! The Frozen Negroni from Capri Club in Los Angeles is bitter, sweet, fruity, and head-freezing. It's very easy to make as long as you have a frozen beverage machine. If you want to impress friends during the warmer months of the year, make this classic cocktail into the best frozen beverage for your next pool party.

\*

**GLASSWARE:** Stemmed ice cream glass

**GARNISH:** Orange slice, maraschino cherry

- 34 oz. Mulholland Gin
- 34 oz. Volume Primo Sweet Vermouth
- 34 oz. Bordiga Bitter (alternative: Campari)
- 34 oz. orange juice
- 34 oz. grapefruit juice
- 25 oz. simple syrup
- 100 oz. water
- 1 teaspoon saline solution (see page 23)

1. Place all the ingredients in a frozen beverage machine and let it freeze.

2. Pour into a stemmed ice cream glass.

3. Garnish with an orange slice and maraschino cherry.

# IL FUTURISTA

L'ANTICA PIZZERIA DA MICHELE NYC
81 GREENWICH AVE, NEW YORK, NY 10014

In the world of pizza, there is no more legendary spot than L'Antica Pizzeria da Michele from Naples. Known for their out-of-this-world Margherita and Marinara pies, the Napoli staple was established in 1870 and has slowly expanded to locations around the globe. One of those locations is in New York City, where they have a one-of-a-kind cocktail program, and luckily, were willing to share one of their unique recipes with me. In their words, "When drinking the Il Futurista, we encourage our guests to take a bite of the Parmigiano Reggiano cheese and then take a sip of the cocktail. The cheese releases the botanical aromas of the gin—juniper, coriander, cardamom, citrus, and lavender. When you bite into the olive the cocktail becomes savory and salty."

---

✳

**GLASSWARE:** Nick & Nora glass, chilled
**GARNISH:** Large Castelvetrano olive, cube of Parmigiano Reggiano cheese

---

- 1 ½ oz. Elena Gin London Dry
- 1 oz. Wodka Vodka

- ½ oz. Antica Torino Dry Vermouth
- 3 drops saline solution (see page 23)

1. Add all the ingredients to a mixing glass with ice and stir until chilled.

2. Strain the cocktail into a chilled Nick & Nora glass.

3. Garnish with a Castelvetrano olive and a cube of Parmigiano Reggiano.

# BROTHER WOLF

When it comes to Italian cocktails, the last place you're probably thinking about is Knoxville, Tennessee. But the fact that one of the best Italian cocktail bars in the United States is located in the South should tell you that something special is happening with Italian products, as they're becoming more and more abundant in the most unlikely of places.

Brother Wolf is an Italian aperitivo bar that is run by Italophiles Jessica "Rabbit" King and Aaron Thompson. "Brother Wolf conjures Italy's beloved aperitivo bars. Beyond great food, wine, and cocktails, we hope to recreate the warm and generous hospitality and sense of community that we encountered in Italy during all of our visits."

The bar is completely unique to Knoxville, and customers have embraced their Italian style and how they wanted to incorporate Italy's tradition of aperitivo—the time before dinner to drink and snack on small bites.

"In Italy, we fell in love with its dining and drinking traditions, the ease at which Italians meet and socialize, and their displays of affection for each other," says King. "There has never been a better time to offer people a relaxed environment to really take time for each other and enjoy the company of friends."

The bar opened in 2021 and was named in *Esquire* as one of the most coveted bars in America in 2022.

"We feel humbled and grateful for Brother Wolf to be so adored by Knoxville and attract the national media spotlight," says King. "It is so gratifying to see Brother Wolf's concept resonating so deeply across a demographic that spans generations. Our guests are fascinated by our cocktails accented by exquisite Italian aperitivi and digestivi, whether in serious stirred drinks or whimsical frozen tipples. It's truly exhilarating to see gin drinkers become Negroni aficionados."

Brother Wolf has one of the most impressive cocktail programs in the country and features a cavalcade of rare and obscure amari, which they use to make dozens of classic and unique Italian drinks like the Hugo (see page 62), and the Il Professore (see page 401).

# IL PROFESSORE

BROTHER WOLF
108 W JACKSON AVE #1, KNOXVILLE, TN 37902

One of the signature cocktails from the Italy-loving team at Brother Wolf in Knoxville, Tennessee, Il Professore takes your taste buds on a bitter and sour journey, but with a final stop of sweetness to cut things down a bit. This drink has three different amari in it—Amaro Montenegro, which is more smooth; Fernet-Branca, which is very bitter; and Cynar, which is less bitter than Branca but is made with artichokes for a really unique flavor profile. These combined with lemon juice and honey syrup are a pure delight. Make this cocktail at home to surprise your guests with something different and definitely order it at Brother Wolf the next time you find yourself in Knoxville.

---

✳

**GLASSWARE:** Coupe glass, chilled

**GARNISH:** Thin peel of lemon

- ¾ oz. Amaro Montenegro
- ¾ oz. Fernet-Branca
- ¾ oz. Cynar
- ¾ oz. lemon juice
- ¾ oz. honey syrup (50:50)

1. Combine all the ingredients in a cocktail shaker and dry-shake for 30 seconds.

2. Add ice and shake for an additional 10 seconds.

3. Strain into a coupe.

4. Garnish with a thin peel of lemon.

# SBAGLIATO ROSSO

## PONTI
### MODENA, ITALY

The name Ponti is practically synonymous with balsamic vinegar. The company has been producing the liquid gold since 1787 and are now run by the ninth generation of the family.

Balsamic vinegar, as you probably know, is incredibly sweet and also incredibly acidic. Because of those properties, it can be tricky to mix into cocktails to both enhance a drink while still getting the essence of the balsamic.

With the popularity of the Negroni Sbagliato, it makes sense that there would be a wide range of variants. Ponti hopped on this train but changed it up with a twist. Instead of prosecco, the recipe calls for Lambrusco from Modena. But the truly inspired difference is the addition of Ponti's cherry condiment, which is a rich and creamy balsamic vinegar with a cherry jam flavor. Bitter, sweet, and bubbly, it's a beautiful pre-dinner cocktail.

**GLASSWARE:** Old-fashioned glass
**GARNISH:** Orange slice, maraschino cherry

- 1 oz. Campari
- 1 oz. Cocchi Vermouth Di Torino
- ½ teaspoon Ponti Cherry Condiment
- 1 oz. Lambrusco di Modena

1. Add the Campari, vermouth, and cherry condiment to an old-fashioned glass filled with ice and stir.

2. Top with the Lambrusco and stir.

3. Garnish with an orange slice and cherry.

# CAFFE MODENA

An Espresso Martini by another name, the Caffe Modena is sweet, chocolaty, and has one hell of a caffeine kick. If you want to ditch Red Bull and vodka at the club, switch to this Ponti-created drink instead. Here you'll get your vodka, but the addition of a sweet coffee liqueur, another sweet chocolate liqueur, espresso, and Ponti's Chili Pepper Glaze will energize this cocktail with spice, bitterness, and a touch of acidity. It looks and tastes as dreamy as it gets.

**GLASSWARE:** Martini glass

**GARNISH:** Three coffee beans

- 1 ½ oz. vodka
- 1 ½ oz. espresso
- ¾ oz. Meletti Cioccolato Liqueur
- ¾ oz. coffee liqueur
- ¼ teaspoon Ponti Chili Pepper Glaze

1. Add all the ingredients to a cocktail shaker with ice and shake vigorously.

2. Strain the cocktail into a martini glass.

3. Garnish with coffee beans.

# IMAGINARY FRIEND

DAMIAN
2132 E 7TH PL, LOS ANGELES, CA 90021

Bear with me for a moment, as this is the last cocktail in the book. Damian is a modern Mexican restaurant in Los Angeles, but at the bottom of its cocktail menu is something just Italian enough. Now, I have to confess something—of every drink I tried and tested in this book, this is the one that I loved the most.

It's a version of a Mezcal Negroni that uses Carpano Bianco, a clear, crisp Italian vermouth with a light profile; Dolin Blanc, a French vermouth that's pale and slightly sweet; Salers Gentian Liqueur, which is a French liqueur with herbal and citrus notes; and Yola Mezcal, which is smoky in aroma, but smooth in flavor. It is the silkiest drink in this whole book, and I hope if you do nothing else, make this, as you'll remember it forever in the same way I do.

**GLASSWARE:** Rocks glass

**GARNISH:** Pineapple guava or finger lime

- 1 ¼ oz. Yola Mezcal
- ½ oz. Carpano Bianco
- ½ oz. Dolin Blanc Vermouth
- ½ oz. Salers Gentian Liqueur

1. Chill a mixing glass.

2. Add a large cube of ice to a rocks glass.

**3.** Add all the ingredients to the mixing glass. Add ice and stir for a slight dilution.

**4.** Strain the cocktail into the rocks glass.

**5.** Garnish with a sliver of fruit on top of the ice cube.

# ACKNOWLEDGEMENTS

I have a lifelong love affair with the country of Italy, and it's this obsession that ultimately led me to write this book.

First, I want to thank my wife, Marisa, for her never-ending support and for putting up with my insanely long hours, trips away, and countless requests for help. Thanks to my son, Leo, who has no idea I'm writing this book, but is there with leg hugs to always keep things balanced like a fine Negroni.

Thanks to Adam Skolnick for all things books all the time. Your insights into writing on every level and your work continue to inspire me, and I can't tell you how much I value our friendship and working relationship. To my family, Kathy, Neal, Andy, Neil, Peggy, Nat, Beverly, and Dennis, thanks for being endlessly supportive of everything I write, and to Meredith for keeping an eye on Leo throughout this process.

My Cider Mills/Harper Collins Team: thank you to Lindy, Buzz, and Jeremy for giving me this unbelievable opportunity and for wading through the 500+ pages I turned in as a first draft.

Thanks to my editor at *La Cucina Italiana*, Carole Hallac, who not only hired me to write hundreds of articles on Italian food and drinks but was indispensable for her Italian contacts. Also, thanks to my editors at *Fodor's Travel* (Jeremy Tarr) and *Travel + Leisure* (Nina Ruggiero) who continue to hire me to write about Italy and helped me ultimately land this book.

My history buffs: Livio Lauro, Katie Parla, David Wondrich, and Giammario Villa. Livio, thank you for lacing this book with so much of your expertise. Katie, thanks for always being my Italian sounding board, guru, and friend. David, thanks for dedicating your life to the history of cocktails and sharing that with me and the world. Giammario, thanks for your insights into aperitivo history and culture.

Thank you to publicists/comms/marketers who put me in touch with countless bars, bartenders, and liquor and liqueur brands. There would literally be no book without you.

Thank you to the ultimate connectors: Francesco Lafranconi, you were invaluable to me for this book. Genny Nevoso, you came through with so many great hookups. Sabrina Cohen, thanks for leading me to your people. Ryan King for your endless rolodex. Laura Lazzaroni for your connections and insights.

To all the bartenders, producers, ambassadors, and historians. I couldn't have done this book without your cooperation and dedication to everything you do: Leonardo Lucano, Leonardo Leuci, Luca Picchi, Dario Comini, Oscar Quagliarini, Stefano Santucci, Robert Fleming, Simone De Luca, Tomasso Cecca, Patrick Pistolesi, Stefano Briganti, Alex Frezza, Giuseppe Gallo, Mariantonietta Varamo, Edoardo Sandri, Linden Pride, Paolo Dianini, Lee Zaremba, Matteo di Ienno, Julian Biondi, Maurizio Urru, Christian Philippo, Francesco Zimone, Michele Rubini, Liz Davar, Jessica King, Roberto Bava, Simona Bianco, Micaela Pallini, Giuseppe D'Avino, Fabio Raffaelli, Lorenzo Marolo, Anna Scudellari, Matteo Bonoli, Rudi Carraro, Claudio Stefani Giusti, Antonio Tarricone, Francesca Nonino, Timothée Prangé, Daniel Schmidt, Stefano Cicalese, Matteo Luxardo, Mauro and Sergio Corbia, and others I'm hoping I didn't forget.

Thanks to my eating and drinking and writing compatriots: Dan Ahdoot, Joubin Gabbay, Julie Tremaine, Seth Cohen, Keats, Stein, Ash, Pfeffer, Maria Konnikova, Baxter Holmes, Amber Gibson, Daniele Uditi, Phil Rosenthal, and all my writer friends in the food and travel trenches—you know who you are.

And finally, to all my Italian brothers and sisters in Los Angeles, Italy, and around the world, I can't thank you enough for inviting this nice Jewish boy to be an adopted member of your Italian family. I love you all.

## ABOUT THE AUTHOR

Paul Feinstein has been writing and editing in Los Angeles and around the world for more than 20 years. He has written travel guides to LA, Bangkok, Tokyo, Florence, Vancouver, and Barcelona and has written for myriad publications including the BBC, *Travel + Leisure*, *Fodor's Travel*, *TIME*, *Zagat*, and more.

Paul is the creator of the comic book *A.R.C.*, published by Image Comics. Paul also co-wrote *Ricettario Volume 1*, a sourdough cookbook, with world-famous chef Daniele Uditi.

In addition to his writing credits, Paul is also a producer on the food/travel show *From Scratch*.

An avid traveler, Paul has been to more than 60 countries, lived in Israel, went to cooking school, and is particularly obsessed with Italy and Japan.

## PHOTO CREDITS

Pages 24–25, 32, 36, 38, 41 by Alberto Blasetti; pages 156–157, 159, 160 courtesy Amaro Montenegro; pages 43, 115, 117 by Andrea Di Lorenzo; page 120 by Anthony J. Rayburn; page 407 by Araceli Paz; pages 218, 220, 222 by Baldoria Handbook Piemonte created and produced by Ernest; pages 252–253 by Brechenmacher & Baumann; pages 28, 90–91, 93, 161, 164, 213, 233, 314, 316 courtesy of Campari Group; pages 78, 167, 168, 171 courtesy of Cocchi;pages 292–292, 295 by Conrad Chia Laguna Sardinia; pages 48, 51, 52 courtesy of Cipriani; pages 360, 363, 364 courtesy of Giusti; pages 349, 350 by Dario Comini; pages 77, 209, 210, 212, 320 courtesy of Disaronno; pages 326–327, 332, 335, 337, 338 courtesy of Drink Kong; pages 367, 369 by Emma Louise Swanson; page 145 courtesy of Fernet-Branca; pages 245, 246, 249 courtesy of Four Seasons Hotel Firenze; pages 97, 98 courtesy of Freni e Frizioni; pages 100, 103, 105 by Giada Paoloni; pages 238, 241, 242 courtesy of Hassler Roma; pages 258–259, 261, 263, 264 courtesy of Hotel de la Ville; pages 274–275, 277, 278 courtesy of Hotel Eden, Dorchestor Collection; pages 286–287, 288, 291 courtesy of Hotel Principe Di Savoia; pages 280–281, 283, 284 courtesy of Hoxton Rome; pages 203, 204, 207 courtesy of Italicus LTD; pages 385, 386 by James Cole; page 303 by Jay Nel-McIntosh; pages 371, 374, 377 by Julian Biondi; page 391 courtesy of L'Antiquario; pages 322, 325 by Linden Pride; pages 108, 139, 140, 143, 306, 309 courtesy of Liquore Strega; pages 266–267, 269 by Lisa Lovari; pages 353–355, 357, 359 courtesy of Locale; pages 133, 135, 137, 311 courtesy of Lucano; page 184 courtesy of Luxardo; page 114 by Marcelo Nizzoli; pages 340, 343, 344 by Marco Dell'Accio; pages 59, 73, 83, 84, 177, 214, 319, by Marisa Lynch; pages 31, 46, 56, 60, 64, 80, 147, 148, 152, 155, 200, 216 by Marisa Lynch & Meredith Stisser; pages 191, 192, 195, 196 courtesy of Marolo; pages 106, 119, 123 courtesy of Martini & Rossi; pages 66–67, 69, 71 by Michele Tamasco; pages 186, 188 by Mr. G Franklin; pages 110–111, 305, 393, 395 by Nathaniel Katzman; pages 127, 129, 131 courtesy of Nonino; pages 175, 178 courtesy of Pallini; page 42 by Phototecnica slr + Andrea Di Lorenzo; page 151 courtesy of Poli Distillerie; pages 403, 404 by Francis Verrall on behalf of Ponti Vinegars; page 297 courtesy of Regina Isabella Resort; pages 94, 163 by Reva Keller; pages 254, 257 by Roberto Salomone; pages 270, 272 courtesy of Rocco Forte Hotels; page 397 by Rossella Pisano; pages 1, 2, 3, 4–5, 6, 10, 12, 14–15, 86–87, 234–235, 298–299 used under official license from Shutterstock.com; pages 45, 74, 225, 226, 228, 230 courtesy of Select; page 63 courtesy of South Made Marketing; page 346 by Stefano Jesi; page 379 by The Salty Shutters; pages 399, 400 by Tommy Blankenship; pages 179, 180, 183, 313 courtesy of Vecchia Romagna; pages 381, 383 courtesy of VeryTaste Media.
absinthe

# INDEX

Vienne
Ivrée
Turin
Genes
Coire
Salzbourg
Oster Reich
(Autriche)
Carinthie
Milan
Pavie
Padoue
Frioul
Aquilée
Esclavonie
Parme
Po
Venise
Florence
Ravenne
Pentapole
Toscane
ITALIE
Corse
Ancône
Spolète
Aleria
ROME
Raguse
Mt. Cassin
Benevent
Bénévent
Pte
Naples
Salerne
Pte
Bari
Tarente
Otrante
Palerme
Sicile
Calabre
Messine
Reggio
Hammamet
Corcyre